# Library Personalization

# Library Personalization

**Dr. V.K.J. Jeevan**

**Ess Ess Publications**

4837/24, Ansari Road, Darya Ganj,
New Delhi-110002
✆ : 23260807, 41563444
Fax : 011-41563334
E-mail: info@essessreference.com
url:http://www.essessreference.com

First Published **2007**



ISBN: 81-7000-500-0

**Rs.600/-**

*Published by:*
**Ess Ess Publications**
4837/24, Ansari Road, Darya Ganj, New Delhi-110 002
Tel: 011-23260807, 41563444 Fax: 011-41563334
E-mail: info@essessreference.com
url: www.essessreference.com

*Printed in India at:*
Printline, New Delhi

*to*

*my research guide* ***Professor P Padhi,***

***Professor R V Raja Kumar,***

***MHRD*** *for sponsoring a TAT project,*

*my* ***father*** *who is most happy that at least one of his children earned Ph.D. like him,*

***Professor Namboodhiri*** *and* ***Dr. Ramachandra*** *who made me realise the value of Ph.D.,*

*and*

*my* ***'dream guides'*** *who said no*

# Preface

This book is a modified and generalized version of my Ph.D. thesis, **"Content Personalization in a Technical Institute Library: A Model for the Indian Institutes of Technology with Special Reference to IIT Kharagpur"**, submitted to Utkal University, Bhubaneswar, which had been undertaken to demonstrate the pragmatic application of information technology to library work. The study was prompted by the success of library personalization projects in the USA and the UK. The different developments emerged out of these projects help users to start with a generic library and by making selections and choices create a personal library with pre-selected and relevant information resources. Also, the user can view the different services offered by the library through a single interface providing links to different services and resources in multiple servers inside and outside the library. It has also been designed to enable faculty members and researchers, busy with teaching and research work, to save the considerable time spent in collecting information rather than using it. Evolution of full text information in electronic format like e-books, e-journals, and web resources along with emerging database and web technology have made it feasible to connect content as per users' subject interests to provide such a personalized service.

Whether it is the different access points provided in the catalogue cards, indexes and bibliographies or the exhaustive search intrinsic electronic databases, the sole objective of libraries has been to search and selectively access the contents stored. Information and its massive growth ahead of the systems for tracking their access alienated many users from useful content, leading to an under use of information in many institutions and libraries. With the advent of electronic full text resources and especially the Internet, the demands of clients have substantially increased. They have also become increasingly concerned that they want a 'Web' like search and access at the click of a link facility for information resources stored in the library also. In short, personalization provides the library with a viable mechanism to manipulate the information base using available technologies so that the library appears as a set of separate smaller libraries to individual users. As a result, users find it more effective and convenient in using their (personal small) library catering to their specific need. In the perspective of a modern library setting, personalization involves dynamically scanning and selectively delivering electronic contents (especially the newly added ones at regular intervals) as per individual user interests (through expressed and observed needs). In the absence of such personal information support, users will be left to fend for themselves and forced to scan the information overload through library OPACs (Online Public Access Catalogues), electronic databases (networked/stand alone, bibliographic and full text) etc. This may often lead to information under-use (the principle of least effort dictating that a person may not spend sufficient time to identify all sources of interest). This will further have a drastic impact on research and teaching output, with the right sources not reaching the right person at the right time, thus leading to duplicate research through ignorance of previous activities in the field. Research not backed by sufficient primary literature has to opt for poor outlets for publication and this will hamper its visibility.

In all service networks, some sort of assembling and de-assembling takes place to deliver the most efficient service possible, subject to the different constraints. In a library setting, different users make recommendations for buying books, subscribing journals, licensing electronic resources, availing ILL/DDS facilities etc., and the library then proceeds with satisfying these varied requirements by cumulating requests of a particular type such as requisitions for new books. Once these materials/services are made available to users, the library has to again establish connection with the right user for the right resource. Such a connection, unthinkable in the paper domain, has been made possible in the electronic scenario due to the advantages of computer-aided information processing tools and technologies, especially after the evolution of web technology aided database tools. Through personalization, the librarian attempts to slice the library according to the interests of individual users so that every user will be able to effectively utilize the resources and services which s/he needs the most.

This book is organized in eight chapters. The first chapter **Introduction** covers **definitions** of content, personalization and library personalization. It also states the **objectives**, **merits** and **limitations** of library personalization and describes the various **information sources** for personalization as well as the major **components** of a library personalization system like content serving system, user interest management system, search engine, and content delivery system. In the second chapter, **Personalization Attempts,** a **summary of past work** undertaken is compiled under different headings like personalization using artificial intelligence, personalization using agents, personalization in e-learning, personalization in e-commerce, personalization in telemedicine, personalization by portals, and personalization by libraries. It also provides an overview of the **Indian research**. Chapter 3 '**Personalization Model for IIT Libraries'** presents the **data collected** from libraries of the different IITs through a questionnaire, in tabular form with analysis. Chapter 4 is about **User Interest Management System** and discusses the relevance of an integrated user interest management system for the successful operation of a library personalization system. Chapter 5 presents **Standardization of Subject Terms**. It highlights the special efforts undertaken as part of the study to standardize the terms used in user profiles for optimum retrieval of the relevant results and describes the standardization achieved for two subjects: Computer Science and Physics. Chapter 6 '**Design and Implementation of Library Personalization System'** describes the implementation of the personalization system at the model site, the Central Library of IIT Kharagpur. Chapter 7 **'Testing, Feedback, Improvement and Maintenance'** covers the post implementation aspects to stabilize, improve and sustain the library personalization system developed. The last chapter, Chapter 8 is about **Findings and Suggestions**. It concludes the study with detailed discussions on utility of the research and applications in other fields. It also highlights the scope for further research, major implications, problems and prospects, and important suggestions like steps to be followed in operating the personalization services such as subscribing to electronic resources, procuring hardware/software, training library users and staff, budget and institutional support etc.

My research supervisor **Prof. P Padhi**, Reader, PG Department of Library & Information Science, Utkal University, Bhubaneswar has given me enough freedom to plan and execute the study, but without failing to give his expert advice whenever I am out of track or I become too idealistic. I am deeply indebted to him for helping me in different ways for the successful conduct of this work. Other teachers of the Department, **Prof. M Mahapatra, Dr. B Parida, Dr. G Mahapatra,** and **Dr. P Jena** were also kind enough to render any help asked for and express due concern for the smooth completion of this research. The staff and students of the Department were always forthright in offering any support as and when asked for.

**MHRD**'s support for a TAT project helped me to implement a working model. **Prof. Raja Kumar** was kind enough to encourage and support me in this as the Principal Investigator of the project. First and foremost, I wish to acknowledge my heartfelt thanks to **Librarians of IITs (Dr. Yogendra Singh, Dr. Jagdish Arora, Dr. B Saibaba**, and **Dr. S P Singh)** who encouraged me in this study by sharing their experiences on the topic by filling up the Questionnaire used in the pre implementation stage of the study. I am also thankful to **Dr. Harish Chandra** and **Dr. Jagdish Arora** for the courtesy extended during my visits to IITs at Chennai and Mumbai. I am thankful to many of the **authors** whose papers I have referred to while conducting this study, since many such papers prompted me to substantially refine my ideas. Respected **Prof. P N Kaula**'s encouraging words regarding the importance of completing PhD was one of the prime motivations for completing this study, despite the delays due to over-involvement in official and academic work. I am thankful to distinguished senior professional **Dr. B M Gupta** of NISTADS, New Delhi, for introducing me to **Prof. P Padhi**. **Prof. M M Kashyap** and **Dr. B K Sen** were kind enough to examine the synopsis and suggest new insight and fresh ideas. **Teachers, friends** and **professional colleagues** deserve special mention for motivating and encouraging me.

My primary gratitude goes to my previous employer, **Indian Institute of Technology Kharagpur**. The Institute authorities were kind enough to grant their valuable permission to undertake this work without disturbing any of my official duties. The successive **Heads of the Institute and the Central Library** whole-heartedly supported my academic endeavours and I would like to personally thank each one of them. I am also happy to note my special thanks to all my **colleagues in the Central Library** whose direct and indirect unstinting help at various stages helped me continue with this work. **Mrs. B S Sirisha**, Project Assistant in the SAI Project, assisted me to proceed with most of the implementations discussed in this study. **Ms. Minoo Lohani**, Ex-Professional Trainee, Central Library, IIT Kharagpur has been a great source of help and useful assistance in different ways in the reporting of this study and I feel no words are sufficient to express my profound gratitude towards her.

Mr. Sumit Sethi and his team at Ess Ess Publications desire special commendation for bringing out this book in a pleasing format at such a short time.

Members of my **family** and **in-laws** deserve special mention for their encouragement and concern. Finally, this research work has now become a reality due to my **wife** and **children** who wholeheartedly supported me in all my academic initiatives even though I was always taking the time meant for them for all such activities.

Delhi **(Dr. V K J Jeevan)**
June 2006

4. Name the second law and the fourth law also.

5. What is the meaning of organism in fifth law [illegible] growth of the library [illegible]

Answers

1. Books are for use. Every reader his book. Every book its reader. Save the time of the reader. Library is a growing organism.

2. The second law is every book its reader in which the emphasis is given to the book.

3. The provisions of fourth law are : Open access, Classification, Cataloguing, Charging system etc.

4. Name of second law is *every reader his book* [illegible] *books in general*.

5. *Organism* means a living being. The library is considered a growing organism which needs to expand [illegible] with its growth and development of its components.

[illegible] Dictionary catalogue gives information about documents available in a library with reference to their authors, titles, subjects etc. The entries are arranged in a single alphabetical order. As all entries are arranged [illegible] arranged in a single alphabetical order it resembles in arrangement of its entries as in a natural language dictionary in which all words are arranged in one single alphabetical order.

1. Dictionary catalogue is one of the types of physical forms or inner forms of the catalogue ?

2. Why it is called dictionary catalogue ?

3. What types of entries are arranged in it ?

4. Whether dictionary catalogue is being displayed in two separate parts ? If yes, what types of entries these two parts contain ?

5. Define dictionary catalogue in your words.

Answer

1. Dictionary catalogue is one of the inner forms of the catalogue.

2. As all types of entries are arranged in it like a dictionary hence it

# Contents

# List of Tables

# List of Figures

# List of Abbreviations

| | |
|---|---|
| AACR II | Anglo American Cataloging Rules Second edition |
| ABI | American Business Information |
| ACM | Association for Computing Machinery |
| AI | Artificial Intelligence |
| AIDA | Artificial Intelligence Document Analysis |
| AIP | American Institute of Physics |
| ALA | American Library Association |
| ASCII | American Standard Code for Information Interchange |
| ASTM | American Society for Testing and Materials |
| ATM | Asynchronous Transfer Mode |
| BCS | Bardeen Cooper Schrieffer |
| BIS | Background Information Services |
| bmp | bit-mapped graphics format |
| CA | Chemical Abstracts |
| CAB | Cambridge Agriculture Bureau, now CAB International |
| CALIBER | Convention on Automation of Libraries in Education and Research Institutions |
| CAD | Computer Aided Design |
| CAS | Current Awareness Service |
| CASE | Computer Aided Software Engineering |
| CCOD | Current Contents on Diskette |
| CD | Compact Disk |
| CD-ROM | Compact Disk Read Only Memory |

| | |
|---|---|
| CHN | Central Library, Indian Institute of Technology Madras, Chennai |
| CIPHER | Communities of Interest Promoting Heritage of European Regions |
| CPR | Computer-based Patient Record |
| CPS | Content Personalization System |
| CR | Content-Recommending |
| CS | Computer Science |
| CSA | Channel Surfing Analysis |
| CSE | Computer Science & Engineering |
| DA | Dissertation Abstracts |
| DDS | Document Delivery Service |
| Dep/Dept | Department |
| DFD | Data Flow Diagram |
| DLH | Central Library, Indian Institute of Technology Delhi, Delhi |
| DPA | Digital Portfolio Archive |
| DOS | Disk Operating System |
| DTV | Digital TeleVision |
| DVD | Digital Video Disc |
| e-books | Electronic books |
| e-journals | Electronic journals |
| E-SDI | Electronic Selective Dissemination of Information |
| EAD | Encoded Archival Description |
| EBL | Explanation-Based Learning |
| ECT | Engineering, Computing and Technology |
| EDUCOSM | Personalized Writable Web for Learning Communities, a project at Helsinki Institute for Information Technology, Finland |
| ELINOR | ELectronic INformation Online Retrieval |

| | |
|---|---|
| emp | Employee/s |
| EUN | Enhanced User Need |
| EXAFS | Extended X-ray Absorption Fine Structure |
| FOCI | Flexible Organizer for Competitive Intelligence |
| GHT | Central Library, Indian Institute of Technology Gauhati, Gauhati |
| gif | Graphics Interchange Format |
| GKRS | Geospatial Knowledge Representation System |
| GUI | Graphical User Interface |
| HTML | Hyper-Text Markup Language |
| HTTP | Hyper-Text Transfer Protocol |
| IBID | India Business Insight Database |
| IBM | International Business Machines |
| ICOLC | International Coalition of Library Consortia |
| ICSTI | International Council on Scientific and Technical Information |
| id | Identifier, identification |
| IDF | Inverse Document Frequency |
| IDS | Intelligent Database System |
| IEE | Institution of Electrical Engineers |
| IEEE | Institute of Electrical and Electronics Engineers |
| IEL | IEEE/IEE Electronic Library |
| IIM | Indian institute of Management |
| IISc | Indian Institute of Science, Bangalore |
| IIT | Indian Institute of Technology |
| ILL | Inter Library Loan |
| INDEST | Indian National Digital Library in Engineering Science and Technology |
| INFLIBNET | Information and Library Network |
| info | Information |

| | |
|---|---|
| INSPEC | Information Service for Physics, Electronics, and Computing |
| IP | Internet Protocol |
| IRM | Internet Relationship Management |
| ISA | Internet Search Advisor |
| ISI | Institute for Scientific Information |
| ISP | Internet Service Provider |
| ISTP | Index to Scientific Technical Proceedings |
| IT | Information Technology |
| ITU-R | International Telecommunication Union Radiocommunication Sector |
| ITU-T | International Telecommunication Union Telecommunication Standardization Sector |
| Jour | Journal |
| K-DIME | Kansei Distributed Information Management Environment |
| KGP | Central Library, Indian Institute of Technology Kharagpur |
| KNP | P K Kelkar Library, Indian Institute of Technology Kanpur, Kanpur |
| KOD | Knowledge on Demand |
| LAN | Local Area Network |
| LANL | Los Alamos National Laboratory |
| LIDAR | LIght Detection And Ranging |
| LIS | Library and Information Science |
| LISA | Library and Information Science Abstracts |
| LS | Life Sciences |
| MB | Mega/Million Bytes |
| MHRD | Ministry of Human Resources Development |
| MIMD | Multiple Instruction Multiple Data |

| | |
|---|---|
| MIT | Massachusetts Institute of Technology |
| MP | Meteorology and Physics |
| MPEG | Moving Picture Experts Group |
| MS | MicroSoft |
| MUM | Central Library, Indian Institute of Technology Bombay, Mumbai |
| NCSU | North Carolina State University |
| NEXAFS | Near-Edge X-ray Absorption Fine Structure |
| NUCSSI | National Union Catalogue of Scientific Serials in India |
| NIT | National Institute of Technology (earlier REC) |
| OOP | Object Oriented Programming |
| OO-RM | Object-Oriented Rule-based Model |
| OPAC | Online Public Access Catalogue |
| OPAL | Online Personal Academic Librarian |
| OS | Operating Systems |
| OU | Open University |
| PACS | Physics and Astronomy Classification Scheme |
| PC | Personal/Desktop Computer |
| PCES | Physics, Chemical and Earth Sciences |
| PDA | Personal Digital Assistant |
| PDF | Powder Diffraction File, Also Adobe Portable Document Format |
| PDL | Personal Digital Library |
| PDR | Personal Digital Recorders |
| Pdetails | Personal Details |
| PG | Post Graduate |
| Per | Person |
| PHP | Hypertext Preprocessor |
| PHY | Physics and Meteorology |

| | |
|---|---|
| PIPE | Personalization is Partial Evaluation |
| Prof. | Professor |
| PSI | Personalized Systems of Instruction |
| PSMS | Personalized Service Management System |
| PVET | Personalized Virtual Exhibition Tour |
| QCD | Quantum Chromodynamics |
| R&D | Research & Development |
| RAM | Random Access Memory |
| REC | Regional Engineering College |
| RKE | Central Library, Indian Institute of Technology Roorkee, Roorkee |
| ROUTES | Resources for Open University TEachers and Students |
| S&T | Science and Technology |
| SAI | Personalized Selective Access Information System |
| SDI | Selective Dissemination of Information |
| SGML | Standard Generalized Markup Language |
| SIG | Special Interest Group |
| SQL | Structured Query Language |
| Sterms | Subject terms |
| TCP/IP | Transmission Control Protocol/Internet protocol |
| TEXPROS | TEXt PROcessing System |
| TINA | Text-INhalts-Analyse |
| TRF | Test Result Feedback |
| TF | Term Frequency |
| UCLA | University of California, Los Angeles |
| UG | Under Graduate |
| URL | Uniform Resource Locator |
| USENET | User's Network, a world-wide distributed discussion system |

| | |
|---|---|
| VLSI | Very Large Scale Integration |
| VSM | Value Stream Mapping |
| Web | World Wide Web, WWW |
| WBI | Web Browser Intelligence |
| XANES | X-ray Absorption Near-Edge Structure |
| XML | Extensible Markup Language |

# Chapter 1
# Introduction

## 1.1. OUTLINE

Libraries since times immemorial have attempted to collect, organize and disseminate information resources of interest to their clients. They use a variety of tools and techniques to effectively conduct these tasks and devise a host of services to support the varied requirements of their users. There were difficulties in achieving one-to-one mapping of information resources and users in the print environment since options to connect the two basically need surrogates like card, indexes, documentation lists etc. The onset of computer and information technology enabled this mapping to be more efficient, especially because of the ease with which a document can be indexed and represented with multiple terms. The same functionality emerged for representing a user's interests, and in most cases having both in the same computerized system facilitated the easy linking of relevant sources to prospective users. With widespread availability of full text information resources such as electronic books, electronic journals and Internet resources, the significance of computer based linking of sources and users has become more pronounced. The accessibility of electronic resources also tempted users to satisfy their information needs beyond the four walls of the library. These two contradicting virtues of electronic information and the presence of information technology tools prompted libraries in the advanced countries to opt for personalization of library resources for maximum user benefit.

**Ranganathan** (1961) has advocated that reference service should establish contact between reader and his documents in a personal way. Having a large collection and adding new documents at regular intervals will defeat the very purpose of a library if they are not being used. Thus libraries involve users in every activity concerning information collection and organization for user interests influencing crucial decisions. These issues have gained added significance especially in the context of information explosion and arrival of electronic information resources. All electronic resources developed, procured or licensed so far cannot provide service to the fullest extent unless a user is well acquainted with the organization of knowledge in that particular resource. This involves concrete strategies and sometimes a personal touch to educate the user about the resource and its features so as to enable him to effectively use it as warranted by the fundamental laws of library science. Here the library personnel involved with operation and servicing of electronic gadgets should come to their rescue. But without prior knowledge of electronic resources, library personnel may not discharge their duties to the expected extent unless they know the tidbits of the content available in electronic resources. A library better organized and well equipped with all the electronic resources cannot do its best for the users without the library staff and users being given personalized attention regarding the availability of information in the electronic resources, the organization of knowledge therein and techniques to handle them. Therefore personal touch in reference service as proposed by Ranganathan holds good in the context of electronic information services to users in the 21$^{st}$ century as well. With this assumption and hypothesis the present study has been undertaken to suggest a viable solution to the problems caused by the explosion of electronic resources in libraries.

There are two categories of users in many of our libraries, loosely regarded as traditional and modern users. It has been found that using electronic resources becomes extremely difficult for the traditional users, and status and prestige often prevents them from approaching library staff and modern users to educate themselves and take advantage of the situation. To eradicate such embarrassment and fear consciousness and bring this category of users to the electronic stream, personalization is required. The emerging information environment also demands considerable proactiveness in professional approach by service centers, the library being no exception. Services like content personalization ease the burden of information search so that the users can spend their time constructively in specialized tasks, thus optimizing the intellectual capital. This also improves the library's image besides boosting the morale of the library staff. In the absence of such services, libraries still hold their traditional look even though equipped with electronic gadgets (as collection only is changed and not services). Consequently, users are left to meet their information requirements on their own, forcing researchers to spend less time for their research activities and leading to duplication of research.

## 1.2. PERSONALIZATION

Since the term personalization gained wide currency especially after the predominance of Web and e-commerce solutions, sources such as ALA Glossary or Encyclopedia of Library & Information Science do not mention this term. Thus we have to depend on definitions coined by current researchers in the area. **Kramer *et al.*** (2000) define personalization as 'a toolbox of technologies and application features; from simple display of the end-user's name on a Web page, to complex catalog navigation and product customization based on deep models of users' needs and behaviors; used in the design of an end-user experience'. **Perugini** and **Ramakrishnan** (2003) define personalization as the automatic adjustment of information content, structure and presentation tailored to an individual user and hence personalizing the user's interaction is the best way to achieve personalization. Personalization chooses content for the user automatically, without direct user request, the process of choosing content remaining hidden. As the system becomes more familiar with user habits by observing behavior, it achieves increased accuracy in predicting future behavior and interests [**Oracle**]. Personalization is a process of gathering and storing information about site visitors, analyzing the stored information and, based on the analysis, delivering the right information to each visitor at the right time [**IBM**]. Personalization in the perspective of a library aims at dynamically selecting and delivering electronic contents as per the expressed as well as observed needs of individual users. Unlike customization where the focus of the content does not change until the user changes it explicitly through another topic selection, personalization chooses content for the user automatically without direct user request, the process of choosing content remaining hidden throughout [oracle]. Personalization thus uses a complex and dynamic set of features for implicit content selection unlike customization which requires explicit user involvement through relatively static and simpler Web site mechanisms. However, the success of a personalization system ultimately depends on its efficacy in mapping user interests and feedback, continuous interactive support received from beneficiaries to sustain and improve its performance, and a large electronic resource base to work with.

## 1.3. LIBRARY PERSONALIZATION

Libraries have been dealing with **content** (information resources) and **users** and consequently have developed various tools and technologies to effectively map content to meet diverse user interests. Content may be anything, including oral language and natural phenomena, which upon observation appears to have a pattern that can be analyzed for descriptive or inferential purposes (**Penland**, 1971). Content describes the information carried by information systems and mass media, and thus makes an important distinction, not always made clear, between the medium and the message. In terms of information systems, content is regarded both as information structured in some way, as a database or (comparatively) unstructured text (**IELIS**, 2003). Content is the meaning that may be assigned to a message (**Satija**, 2004). Any pertinent source of information that may be of interest or use to any client may be termed as 'content' in the perspective of the emerging print plus electronic hybrid library attached to a higher education or research institution. It also assumes a wider connotation in the emerging digital environment since it encompasses both formal (published) sources as well as informal (meant for private distribution in academic circles only) sources irrespective of their physical form (in hard disk/floppy, on CD-ROM, or as web pages) and media (ASCII/scanned text, voice, images, pictures etc.). Content management basically includes the operations of collection, processing, organization, query based retrieval etc.

Whether it is the different access points provided in the catalogue cards, indexes and bibliographies or the exhaustive search intrinsic electronic databases, the sole objective has been to search and selectively access the contents stored. Information and its massive growth ahead of the systems for tracking their access alienated many users from useful content, leading to an under use of information in many institutions and libraries. With the advent of electronic full text resources and especially the Internet, the demands of clients have substantially increased. Many of them now want a 'Web' like search and access at the click of a link facility for information resources stored in the library itself. In today's competitive Web services environment, customer satisfaction and growth do not necessarily guarantee continued usage or retention, with users becoming increasingly demanding as their knowledge and expectations grow [**Myopenlibrary**]. In this scenario, personalization is one application, in theory, to improve the users' overall on-line experience [*ibid.*]. Personalization of library resources is projected as a viable alternative to tide over the information explosion and to conserve the time of users for more productive intellectual tasks. It is thus a natural corollary of the aftermath of large quantum of e-information available and functional web technologies to efficiently manipulate them as per individual user needs. In short, personalization provides the library with a viable mechanism to manipulate the information base using available technologies so that the library appears as a set of separate smaller libraries to individual users. As a result, they find it more effective and convenient using their (personal small) library catering to their specific need.

Easy search and access features associated with electronic information facilitated many service providers to profile and select contents based on various attributes of the service seekers. The technological advancements characterizing web-based computing and the continued interest of users to gather information resources on the web enabled many popular portals to personalize their contents to suit varied user interests. Apart from libraries, several other service providers too resort to personalization to attract more users and site visitors. Electronic commerce and related applications are also increasingly focusing on identifying and recognizing individual users. This enables information regarding services of user interest to be provided to potential clients in a targeted manner at frequent intervals, leading to a substantial increase in both the volume of use and number of satisfied customers. Apart from selecting contents, some services also provide options for selecting the appearance of pages like background colours, fonts, order of menus etc. In the perspective of a modern library setting, content personalization involves dynamically scanning and selecting delivering electronic contents (especially the newly added ones at regular intervals) as per individual user interests (through expressed and observed needs). This may seem to be very similar to typical library services such as Current Awareness Services (CAS) or Selective Dissemination of Information (SDI) services. However, the major difference lies in the attempt to map and provide full text information rather than mere surrogates like indexes or abstracts, increased application of web technology to gather user interests, and selective search and delivery of information ahead of user demand in keeping with specific user requirements.

The basic reasons behind library personalization (**Jeevan** and **Padhi**, 2002) must be:

* Non use of large amounts of contents procured

* Improper use of a small part of contents acquired
* Difficulty in satisfying user demands otherwise
* Difficulty in attracting users to library otherwise
* Easy personalization options for electronic content
* Efficient Collection Management
* Improvement in image of the library

### 1.3.1. Objectives of Library Personalization

In tune with many of the lofty goals of electronic information services, digital libraries and other new breeds of library solutions, most personalization projects underway identified high ideals and exciting goals such as:

* To create a personalized digital library environment that will support the information needs of clients.
* To provide a seamlessly integrated and personalized interface for effective user access to resources of interest at one place without navigating through multiple interfaces and information sources.
* To reduce information overload.
* To facilitate users in spending less time looking for information and more time using it

### 1.3.2. Merits of Library Personalization

In the absence of personal information support, users (especially researchers who work under extreme pressure to deliver solutions regarding consultancy and Research & Development (R&D) projects) will be left to fend for themselves and forced to scan the information overload through library OPACs (Online Public Access Catalogues), electronic databases (networked/stand alone, bibliographic and full text) etc. This may often lead to information under-use (the principle of least effort dictating that a person may not spend sufficient time to identify all sources of interest). This will further have a drastic impact on research and teaching output, with the right sources not reaching the right person at the right time, thus leading to duplicate research through ignorance of previous activities in the field. Research not backed by sufficient primary literature has to opt for poor outlets for publication and this will hamper its visibility. The key merits of library personalization are several. The inherent benefits of such a service include:

* Timesaving, as implied in the fundamental laws of library science
* High quality services and productive work culture as warranted by the latest management principles and practices expected from service institutions

Attempts towards 'information filtering' are always a major area of research in the discipline since information explosion and its aftermath - a flood of sources - indirectly alienate a large number of potential users from a considerable chunk of core resources. A personalized library model:

* Instills more responsibility upon various stakeholders since it is role based (learner, teacher, staff)
* Provides customizable options to choose between the items to be displayed, or more importantly, items not to be displayed
* Is proactive as it allows librarians to send users messages or information on a regular basis
* Is focused as personalization allows listing of only the needed information, and hence users are not flooded with "noise".
* Facilitates creation of users' own web interfaces to a library's information resources in which they can even create a personal work area to annotate and supplement the information resources for personal use
* Promotes the library as a valuable catalyst for change

### 1.3.3. Limitations of Library Personalization

Despite these obvious advantages, however, there are also

certain limitations of personalization as enumerated below:

* A good personalization system aims to connect the user and resource with the help of a match obtained after representing both in a search engine. If the representations fail to properly map the resource/user, results from the personalization system may lead to noise, hampering its utility and affecting users' confidence to utilize the same.
* Factors such as indifference regarding the inclusion of personalization as one of the services, lack of infrastructure/cooperation from the concerned authorities, and inadequate funds/staff may inhibit personalization of library contents for effective user service.

## 1.4. INFORMATION SOURCES FOR PERSONALIZATION

Some of the personalized services offered such as details about books issued, renewed, and reserved by users through the library automation system, electronic notice boards to discuss events and academic activities in the institute etc., need not require subject specialization from the users. Hence, these can be offered without any direct input, unlike services like OPAC of library holdings, email contacts to librarians and other staff, recommendations for book and journal purchases, requests for ILL/DDS services etc., which require different types of user input depending on the information need at a particular instant. Services utilizing a semi-manual or manual approach need to be automated in the first place to interface them with the personalization system. Availability of electronic databases, web access to subscribed and consortia journals and intranet serving of several electronic components have promoted a sufficient quantity of electronic resources in many of our academic and research libraries. Further, coupled with the rapid advances and interest in digital libraries, there is an increasing presence of an institutional digital library facility on the intranet to encompass at one place in-house teaching and research information such as lecture notes, question papers, preprints of publications, theses and dissertations, proceedings of conference hosted by the Institution, reports of R

& D and consultancy projects undertaken etc. The only requirement in the emerging context is to properly frame patron interests and connect them with internal and external (procured and accessed) electronic information to generate personalized alerting and selective retrieval.

Out of the various services offered by different personalization projects in libraries in advanced countries, libraries attached to premier educational and research institutions already have the following:

* Patron information regarding books issued, renewed and reserved by users from OPAC of library holdings, aided by the library automation system
* E-journal access to subscribed and consortia journals from publishers' websites, facilitated through links from library Website or managed through portals like j-gate/Ingenta
* Standalone and networked access to bibliographic and full text CD databases
* Email contacts with librarians and other staff regarding queries about various activities
* ILL/DDS services handled in a manual or semi-electronic form, largely for printed sources
* Recommendations for book and journal purchases through signed manual forms due to purchase formalities
* Electronic notice boards to discuss events and academic activities taking place in the Institute concerned
* Information regarding courses, lecture notes etc., put up by some faculty members on their personal Websites
* Electronic submission of theses

## 1.5. COMPONENTS OF A LIBRARY PERSONALIZATION SYSTEM

Personalization needs sufficient electronic content at one's site as well as suitable mechanisms to identify the user through his/her profile, selectively search the content that matches the user profile, and arrange and present it to the user in an appealing fashion. The different components of a content personalization system include:

* **Content Serving System** to host electronic content beyond a critical mass
* **User Interest Management System** to manage dynamic user profiles
* **Search Engine** to automatically match content over profiles
* **Personalized Content Delivery** mechanisms for delivering matched results to the user.

### 1.5.1. Content Serving System

Libraries attached to academic and research institutions in general and technical libraries in particular are experiencing the virtues of electronic information in the form of e-journals, e-books, bibliographic/full text electronic databases in CD/through web access, and so on (Jeevan and Padhi). Even before the advent of the Indian National Digital Library in Engineering Science and Technology (INDEST) consortium, for ex., the Central Library of IIT Kharagpur was able to provide electronic access to over 600 of the 1000 plus journals subscribed to in print. Apart from this, there are also full text databases such as IEEE/IEE Electronic Library (IEL) and standards. Though these provide enough full text coverage in addition to book CDs, e-books and web information, it is a fact that Current Awareness Service/ Selective Dissemination of Information (CAS/SDI) services have so far not included the full text databases, either due to differences in file formats or technical difficulties in handling full text information (Jeevan and Padhi). A similar situation regarding electronic full text information is present in the other IITs too. Now with the help of INDEST Consortium, access to e-resources has increased from the present level of access to e-journals from 100 to 500 to more than 4000 journals in case of IITs and IISc. This is comparable to world class institutions like MIT (**Arora** and **Agrawal**) and clearly indicates the presence of substantial amount of formal content in the IITs, which could effectively be used for personalization services. Further, inclusion of in-house or local contents and informal contents on the Web will lead to a substantially larger body of useful information for serious researchers in these institutions.

### 1.5.2. User Interest Management System

Library Science works on the principle of classifying and arranging information resources of interest to users and devising effective and efficient techniques for their selective retrieval. Thus profiling users to manage user interests is as important as collection development and access management activities. In a library, apart from collection and staff, the user is the vital link in the information consumption chain, the other two existing only for the user. A typical personalization scheme may take any or all of the user Web-surfing patterns, past use statistics, past user ratings of items, anticipated nature and degree of user interest, and user demographics, such as qualifications, field of interest. professional interests etc., into account [Myopenlibrary].

So far, user interest management in libraries has not been taken up in an integrated manner due to the diversity of electronic systems used, forcing the recorded user interests to remain scattered (Jeevan and Padhi). The library automation system holds a complete inventory of books issued, returned, renewed and reserved by a user, as well as user/department profiles for CAS/SDI of current books. CAS/SDI services for journal articles are operated with the help of an electronic bibliographic database using detailed user profiles or user groups in the proprietary software of the database. Recommendations from individual users are seriously sought and considered for procuring books, and such recommendations on a departmental/group of department basis definitely influence addition or deletion of journals. However, since user recommendations and preferences stand only in the concerned automation software modules or native software systems, they fail to give an integrated picture of user interests.

While constructing user profiles, apart from expressed needs, many do not consider important (most likely due to difficulty in recording) usage statistics and use behaviour observable from library databases, records kept at ILL/Resource Sharing unit, Reprography Section etc., (Jeevan and Padhi).

### 1.5.3. Search Engine

A search engine is vital as better results could be mined from the content servers using profile terms, depending on the efficacy of the search facility. Technical obstacles concerning searching from proprietary systems only using native search engines may impede library centered solutions for concurrent searching of multiple databases. Currently, a modern technical library has to work with different proprietary search engines of individual electronic resources such as Science Direct of Elsevier Science, Digital Library of ACM, IEL of IEEE etc., as per the existing licenses. Copying bibliographic data of interest to local users with the full text link from the different services in a local database system could be another option. The same database can also hold metadata and even full text of internal digital resources so that concrete coverage of resources is possible.

### 1.5.4. Personalized Content Delivery

In a wired campus where everyone is comfortably familiar with Information Technology (IT), content delivery in electronic form is the obvious choice. However, sending content by email, though easy, is equally discouraging in the present day spam dominated email scenario. Creating personal pages for researchers on the personalization server and alerting them about new postings (obviously through email as and when required) would be the ideal option.

## 1.6. OBJECTIVES AND LIMITATIONS OF THE STUDY

### 1.6.1. Objectives

* To critically explore and survey the attempts made so far in selectively providing information to library users.

* To evolve a suitable framework for personalized information delivery to the library's clients, utilizing the latest research techniques of information science.
* To evolve a model for library personalization in the perspective of Indian libraries.
* To implement a prototype for content personalization.

### 1.6.2. Limitations

Such specialized studies are to be undertaken in a focused manner rather than incorporating a large number of institutions in a single study. Since IITs represent institutions of world class standard in the country and their libraries regarded as supreme as far as resources and services are concerned, this study has taken IIT libraries as a model for assessing and testing localized effects required for the study. Since the system will have an automatic work-environment, only electronic resources may be brought under its purview, to begin with. Thus printed resources are excluded from the consideration of the study. Also, since the users in an educational institute are largely students who are a floating population, the study will first attempt to map the interests of faculty and researchers only in order to create a substantial interaction between users and resources. Also, the user profiles are constructed from keywords suggested by the users themselves and are thus restricted by inadequate expression of information requirements of need, want etc. from the user point of view. In some cases users are too involved with their academic work to provide suitable input, and hence the library has to collect keywords from alternate sources such as homepages, department/ Institute Web sites, Annual/Research reports or keywords from their publications. Further, the need expressed is not always the actual need. Thus efforts are also being made to observe individual use patterns as significant input to enable intelligent profile modification process. In this context, though the library automation system returns results of whatever sources have been issued by users, it is difficult to quantify what sort of books are being read in the reading rooms and to identify which articles are photocopied. We will discuss some attempts at personalization in the next chapter.

**REFERENCES**


1. **IBM**, http://www-4.ibm.com/software/developer/library/personalization/
2. **IELIS**, Feather (John) and Sturges (Paul), *Ed.* International Encyclopedia of Library & Information Science. Routledge, London. 2003. p 105-106.
3. **Jeevan** (V K J) and **Padhi** (P). Towards Personalising the Electronic Contents in Technical Libraries. *University News*. 40; 21; May 27- June 2, 2002; 3-9.
4. **Kramer** (Joseph) et al. A User-Centered Design Approach to Personalization. *Communications of the ACM.* 43; 8; August 2000; 45-48.
5. **Myopenlibrary**, http://library.open.ac.uk/aboutus/myolib/introduction.htm
6. **Oracle**, http://otn.oracle.com/tech/java/oc4j/doc_library/902/tagut/personal.htm
7. **Penland** (Patrick R.). Content analysis. *In* Encyclopedia of Library & Information Science. Marcel Dekker, New York, 1971.V5, p 633.
8. **Perugini** (S) and **Ramakrishnan** (N). Personalizing Web sites with mixed-initiative interaction. *IT Professional*. 5; 2; March-April, 2003; 9 – 15.
9. **Ranganathan** (S R). Reference Service. Asia Publishing, Bombay, 2nd ed., 1961 p 53.
10. **Satija** (M P). A dictionary of knowledge organization. Amritsar: Guru Nanak Dev University, 2004. p 50.

# Chapter 2
# Personalization Attempts

## 2.1. PERSONALIZATION USING ARTIFICIAL INTELLIGENCE

**Zhu** *et al.* (1999) present a Geospatial Knowledge Representation System (GKRS) prototype that integrates multiple knowledge sources (textual, image, and numerical) to support concept-based geographic information retrieval. Based on semantic network and neural network representations, GKRS loosely couples different knowledge sources and adopts spreading activation algorithms for concept based knowledge inferencing. **Matthijssen** (1998) has laid out the architecture of an information system in which task model index is based on a model of legal tasks as opposed to traditional database indexes to represent database contents for determining the information need, retrieving relevant documents and offering methodical guidance for the legal task. Research on case-based reasoning has explored the concept of retrieval and adaptation of previous experience in the form of cases, the retrieval process using an index vocabulary to capture both the content and context of previous cases. Current approaches to empirical evaluation of case-based reasoning systems often do not consider the crucial role a content-oriented index vocabulary plays in the various stages of the case-based reasoning process, evaluating a case-based discovery system and proposing a general schema for content-oriented evaluation of case based reasoning systems (**Oehlmann**, 1998). **O'Leary** (1998) examines the use of artificial intelligence in knowledge management, focusing on the artificial intelligence-related technologies of knowledge bases (as content of the knowledge management system) and ontologies (as context of knowledge management). **Shukla** (1996) mentions some state of the art techniques for online information retrieval over the Internet, provides some guidelines for the design of new intelligent search techniques, presents an intelligent search algorithm and discusses Artificial Intelligence (AI) techniques for content based image retrieval using evolutionary programming for feature extraction and object recognition. The critical role of artificial intelligence in a digital library is to provide an infrastructure that accommodates extreme heterogeneity of content and function, while supporting continual extension and evolution in both categories.

**Cosinger** (1994-95) describes a user model needed to support runtime determination of form and content, and an approach to the acquisition, representation and exploitation of user models: the most plausible user model being the result of an abductive recognition process which incorporates assumptions about the user which are then used to constrain the design. **Armengol** and **Plaza** (1995) analyze six different explanation-based machine-learning (EBL) methods and provide an overview of where the descriptions of EBL methods are realized at the knowledge level. Knowledge level description is a proposal that emphasizes the knowledge content and usage and abstracts away implementation details (**Armengol** and **Plaza**, 1995). **Zarri** (1994) presents the main phases of conceptual parsing strategy able to produce, through a rule-based approach and in a (largely) automated way, representation of natural language texts. **Savoy** (1993-94) suggests a new retrieval model where documents are represented according to both their content and relationships with other sources of information. **Schuegraf** and **Bommel** (1993) mention a design, combining both statistical and artificial intelligence techniques, of an automatic indexing system based on two cooperating expert systems which examines choice of content indicators, the effect of stemming and the identification of characteristic vocabularies for given subject areas. The AIDA project was set up with assistance from the Australian government to develop automated document analysis techniques such as point form summaries and keyword generation output either as separate documents or in a hypertext structure (**Jones** and **Corbett**, 1992). Whereas document analysis was mainly concerned with the handling of formal properties of documents (scanning, editing etc.), AI techniques in the field of natural language processing have shown the possibility of 'content based text handling', i.e. content analysis for textual documents as described by **Schwarz**. This relates to various linguistic software tools in the field of intelligent text handling developed at the Siemens Corporate Research Laboratories, as part of the TINA project (Text-Inhalts-Analyse—text content analysis). The design of sophisticated information systems is analyzed in terms of five system characteristics: subject matter and source of content, development of the internal representation, form(s) of the representation, types of queries allowed, and 'world knowledge' in the representation. A series of prototype full-text/graphics systems is being developed, the first answering queries by literal string matching and the most advanced answering complex queries using computational linguistic and AI techniques (**Futrelle** and **Smith**, 1982).

There are adaptive algorithms (genetic algorithms and neural networks) in clustering hypermedia documents as these clusters allow the user to index into the nodes and find information quickly. The clustering focuses on the user's paths through the hypermedia document and not on the content of the nodes or the structure of the links in the document, the clustering thus reflecting the unique relationships each user sees among the nodes. The original hypermedia document remains untouched, with each user having a personalized index into this document (**Johnson** and **Fotouhi,** 1995), (**Johnson** and **Fotouhi,** 1996). Another approach to bookmark organization provides automatic classification through clustering along with user adoption (**Maarek** and **Shaul**, 1996). **Chen** (1999) proposes an Intelligent

Database System (IDS) capable of dynamically restructuring a relational database to adapt to changes for providing timely query response and satisfactory database information-retrieval performance. To achieve this objective, a sequence of methodologies was developed to classify queries of different complexity levels, identify high-performance robust database structures, consider system congestion conditions and detect query patterns (**Chen**, 1999). **Li** (1999) describes a system to support a complete procedure for automatic document classification and extraction, beginning with the scanning of the paper document into the system and ending with an effective digital form of the original document as output. This is a general-purpose system with 'learning' ('logical closeness' segmentation method) ability and can be adapted easily in many application domains (**Li**, 1999).

**Wu** (1999) analyzes the relative strengths and weaknesses of different data mining techniques and uses one data set to test three classification techniques: decision trees, logistic regression and neural nets, with commonly available software packages, comparing the performances and results of these techniques. Most document processing systems today apply AI technologies to support their system intelligent behaviors, but the core problem is how to represent and manage different kinds of knowledge to support their inference engine components' functionalities, with knowledge management becoming a critical issue in the document processing systems (**Wu**, 1999). **Cao** (1998) presents an integrated overview on the data mining techniques developed recently and reviews the kinds of knowledge to be mined, including association rules, characteristic rules, classification rules, discriminant rules, clustering rules, evolution rules and deviation rules along with challenging issues and emerging algorithms. The available tools, borrowed from several disciplines like databases, statistics, pattern recognition and machine learning of AI, and visualization, are examined as a hierarchical tree, while other related issues on data cleaning, complexity and privacy are also discussed (**Cao**, 1998). With an increasingly greater number of texts being stored on-line rather than solely in print, an opportunity exists to utilize the power of the computer to aid in the location and analysis of knowledge in on-line texts. **Kavanagh** (1995) proposes one such tool, the Text Analyzer, which combines methods from computational linguistics and artificial intelligence to provide users with a variety of options for finding information in documents, at the same time verifying the consistency of this information by word and conceptual analyses and other operations.

## 2.2. PERSONALIZATION USING AGENTS

**Miao** *et al.* (2002) use fuzzy cognitive agents to provide personalized suggestions based on users' current personal preferences, other users' common preferences, and an expert's domain knowledge. Fuzzy cognitive agents are able to represent knowledge via extended fuzzy cognitive maps, learn users' preferences from most recent cases, and help them make inferences and decisions through numeric computation instead of symbolic and logic deduction. **Liu** *et al.* (2001) propose an integrated framework using XML-based metadata models, user models and agents to develop personalized e-catalogs with a multi-level architecture to facilitate resource discovery and format translation, and can model the definitions of diverse attributes in a flexible manner using three-level user profiles to model users' shopping interests into resources, categories and goods. **Shibata** *et al.* (2002) propose a method of implementing active autonomous agents that discover and recommend contents matching with user preferences by observing user reactions to agent recommended contents without user guidance. The University of Michigan Digital Library Project, USA, aims to satisfy these criteria utilizing an architecture based on distributed information agents (**Wellman** *et al.*, 1996).

**Kim** *et al.* (2002) study the strengths and weaknesses of WebPersonalizer, an agent-based end-user personalization tool and AntWorld, a collaborative recommendation tool, as a Web personalization assistant. Instead of trying to address the information overload problem with search engines and robots (spiders), **Bogonikolos** *et al.* (1999) argue that each server should facilitate by itself the retrieval of desired information published on its own domain through an intelligent agent to provide intelligent, adaptive and personalized navigation within a web server, "Archimides" which undertakes the task of performing intelligent information retrieval, and afterwards to construct a personalized version of the server in the form of an index with links that are dynamically inserted or deleted according to users' interests, preferences and behavior. **Bianchi-Berthouze** and **Kato** (2000) propose a framework for endowing a software agent with the capacity to personalize itself to its users through interaction, and to perform tasks involving subjective factors. They further describe K-DIME, a software prototype that can retrieve web material based on both objective and subjective content features.

**Kantamneni** and **Narayanan** (2001) present a distributed agent architecture that allows for individual agents to collaborate with each other and assist other agents by utilizing user profiles with knowledge of the topic in question and collaborate with users to identify the contextual framework for their specific information requirements. **Xingshe** *et al.* (2003) have devised a multi-agent system to provide personalized and private service in PDRs (Personal Digital Recorders). The steps include observing users' viewing behaviors in the background, continuously updating user profiles, providing different programs for different users according to their respective profile information, protecting users' privacy utilizing XML encryption of reported information and verifying user name and password before reporting his/her profile to the service provider. **Jain** and **Anjum** (2000) have developed an extremely simplified analytical model that examines the claimed performance benefits of mobile agents over client-server computing for a mobile information retrieval scenario. It infers that mobile agents are not necessarily better than client-server calls in terms of average response times;

they are only beneficial if the space overhead of the mobile agent code is not too large, or if the wireless link connecting the mobile user to the fixed servers of the virtual enterprise is prone to error.

## 2.3. PERSONALIZATION IN E-LEARNING

**Cheong** *et al.* (2002) describe the design and implementation of a web-based collaborative enabled multimedia content authoring and management system (CMCAMS) for organizing, integrating and composing personalized and interactive course notes for online education. This system enables educators to manage personalized learning materials that are structured, profiled and streamed to students. It further examines user profiles to identify the level of difficulty to be incorporated and the presentation style to be adopted, based on the bandwidth available. **Dahn** and **Schwabe** (2002) mention the 'Slicing Book approach' for offering personalized electronic textbooks for learners where books are split into slices and the logical relationship between them made explicit, e.g. which slice builds on the knowledge provided by which other slices. This knowledge can then be matched with a model of the users' knowledge to provide them with a personalized textbook. **Tang** *et al.* (2000) propose a method to construct personalized courseware by building a personalized Web tutor tree and mining both context and structure of the courseware to adapt the teaching in accordance with individual students' ability in a distance learning environment. **Hawryszkiewycz** (2003) suggests that software agents assist learners create a personalized life-long learning environment for a specified need using reusable learning objects. Since the existing learning systems have some inbuilt defects in the way learning resources are organized and do not support personalized learning, **Xiao** *et al.* (2001) discuss how to provide learners with a personalized intelligent and interactive learning environment with the aid of learning resources, user model and a resource agent built for the tune-up and integration of Web resources.

**Carchiolo** *et al.* (2003) outline a course generation/ presentation engine which allows the creation of personalized learning paths by extracting lessons, eliminating the ones known to the student, and arranging them into a tree including all possible paths starting from the student's possessed knowledge towards desired knowledge. **Qu and Shen** (2002) introduce an adaptive distance learning mechanism to provide the desired learning resources by analyzing and mining the current personalized data. After getting users' knowledge framework according to the whole knowledge space, it would then take adequate complementary action in the user knowledge framework. **Koyama** *et al.* (2001) propose an agent-based personalized distance learning system which can deliver the learning materials as well as test the learner's understanding. **Hicks** (2002) describes a customization architecture specifically designed for knowledge workers to help them find, access and work with the required information to perform their tasks in a collaborative setting. **Hsu** *et al.* (2003) have evolved a test result feedback (TRF) model that analyzes the relationship between student learning time and corresponding test result to give the instructor crucial information for course content refinement. It can also suggest the student a personalized make-up course or appropriate advanced courses for further study without interfering with student learning and/or increasing the instructor working load. **Karagiannidis** *et al.* (2001) present the development of an architecture for defining reusable adaptive educational content which can be easily interchanged and reused across different personalized learning applications and services, as part of the European Project "Knowledge on Demand" (KOD). **Quarati** (2003) proposes a methodology that combines re-use techniques with personalization for realizing content best fitting the actual needs of different students engaged in diverse learning scenarios and a layered modeling process for personalizable educational content to be used by Web learning communities. **Dadarlat** *et al.* (2002) comment on the possibilities of using the web for course delivery and review techniques for the use of

Personalized Systems of Instruction (PSI) in the Web based course design. EDUCOSM focuses on the possibilities of collaboration and the open-ended nature of the Web with features like sharing and annotation of arbitrary Web-pages, and an adaptive desktop for accessing the evolving contents of the system in a real Web-based course (**Miettinen** ***et al.***, 2003). **Panteleyev** *et al.* (2002) present an approach to constructing a personalized learning program based on Semantic Web technologies by identifying and describing five layers of ontologies needed in future e-learning systems. **Yu** *et al.* (2004) develop a probabilistic framework for finding principled solutions to known problems of recommender systems. The probabilistic active learning method can be used to actively query the user, thereby solving the "new user problem" and reducing the computational cost by working on a carefully selected subset of user profiles while retaining high accuracy. **Schraefel** *et al.* (2000) provide initial reports on a project engaged in developing online collaborative workspaces for dispersed research teams to build virtual communities and personalization within a collaborative environment intended as a "virtual campus". **Papanikolaou** and **Grigoriadou** (2003) propose an instructional framework unifying the lesson generation process, the development of the domain model and the individualized navigation and study support for supporting personalized learning in the context of Web-based adaptive educational hypermedia systems. The framework uses a learning-focused approach that accommodates learning style preferences and progress during interaction. **Zhang** *et al.* (2004) propose three types of navigations for Web-based learning, viz. heuristic tool-using navigation, traffic light progress navigation and suggestive review navigation.

## 2.4. PERSONALIZATION IN E-COMMERCE

**Kun-Lung Wu** *et al.* (2001) describe a prototype system using content-based collaborative filtering techniques to generate dynamic user profiles, form user communities and suggest recommendations for personalization applications. These range from targeted advertising, product or content recommendations to user community services where the system analyzes user logs, fetches the documents accessed and categorizes them. Accordingly each user is described by a vector of document categories. **Ha** (2002) illustrates a Web-based personalization system using both collaborative filtering and Web usage mining to provide online shoppers with the personalized recommendations they need for more intelligent product purchase. **Yu** (1999) examines new developments in data mining and its applications to personalization (tailoring the Web site, advertisement and/or product promotion to a customer based on his past behavior and inference from other like-minded people) in e-commerce (one-to-one marketing instead of the traditional mass marketing) and the need to perform clustering and searching in very high dimensional data space with huge amount of data. By integrating wireless, video, speech and real-time data access technologies, **Asthana** and **Krzyzanowski** (1994) have developed a unique shopping assistant service for personalizing the attention provided to a customer based on individual needs, without limiting his movement, or causing distractions to others in the shopping center. This is achieved with the aid of a centralized server holding the customer database and store database and providing audio/visual responses to inquiries from scores of customers through a very high volume hand-held wireless communications device in real-time over a small area wireless network. **Kim** *et al.* (2003) propose a framework for negotiation processes that provides a consistent model for supporting a comprehensive range of negotiations in dynamic e-commerce environment for successful formation of supply networks and personalized fulfillment of requests.

**Niu** *et al.* (2002) present a new approach to building online customer profiles utilizing three steps: the basic profile, preference profile and rule profile based on the product hierarchy for more effective personalization in electronic commerce where two kinds of real-time recommendations can be generated:

interest recommendation and association recommendation. **Narayanan** *et al.* (2002) describe the design and evaluation of task-based personalized search forms using questionnaire responses, field studies of real-world professionals and cognitive modeling techniques to collect data about the complex information-seeking process under real conditions, develop a knowledge base for principled design, and create a cognitive model of information seeking in a corporate environment. **Schubert** (2000) considers 'Virtual Communities of Transaction' an important arena to realize business potential of the Internet since they can grow trust, cultivate a collective awareness and stress community knowledge, thereby emerging as a valuable component of e-commerce sites, and proposes an architecture for an "enhanced electronic product catalog" with personalized approach using collaborative filtering to alter the interface and the underlying data store. **Youm** and **Cho** (2001) determine a user's item purchasing pattern and recommend the product(s) he/she wants while suggesting an item dependency map which express the relation between purchased items, whereby using an algorithm one can recommend an item a user has not bought yet, but is likely to be interested in.

## 2.5. PERSONALIZATION IN TELEMEDICINE

Using the online patient record as a sophisticated, preexisting user model, **McKeown** *et al.* (2003) have personalized a medical digital library and reranked the search results to prioritize those better matching patient records and highlighting information relevant to patients under the physicians' care. This is particularly beneficial in personal healthcare, where the emphasis has shifted away from acute medical treatment and towards comprehensive disease management based on established practice guidelines, treatment algorithms and/or clinical pathways. This leads to the creation of a next generation computer-based patient record (CPR) providing access to patients' lifelong medical data in a cohesive, distributed manner. Such systems would communicate directly with patients about those actions through the Internet via email, telephony, paging and other available means (**Andonyadis**, 2000).

## 2.6. PERSONALIZATION BY WEB PORTALS

Technological advancements made by web enabled computing coupled with continued user interest to gather information resources available on the web led many popular portals to bring in the concept of content personalization to suit varied user interests. Apart from selecting content, some services also provide options like background colours, fonts, order of menus etc. to select the appearance of pages. **Bradley** discusses the currently popular trend of many leading search engines offering personalized content in the form of 'My XYZ' (for example *My Altavista*, *My Yahoo!, My Excite* and *My Lycos*), in which subject content is arranged under broad headings like business, technology, world news, sports etc.

### 2.6.1. Personalization Services offered by Rediff

Rediff.com provides personalization services covering news personalization, matchmaking, astrology, shopping, etc [**Rediff**]. It allows users to personalize the site by selecting contents such as movies (actors, actresses, other personalities and general events), cricket and sports (badminton, chess, cricket, golf, hockey, motor racing, soccer, tennis etc.), news (political parties, politics and national security), business (industries and market, companies, economy (macroeconomics, markets and exchanges, economic policy and international trade)), columnists, regions (India -states and union territories, neighbouring countries, USA and UK). The contents are selected using the add/remove option in the text boxes provided along with the different categories and subcategories.

### 2.6.2. My Yahoo!

A user can access personalized My Yahoo! pages by choosing both the exact information needed from dozens of different information tools on offer (news, calendar, email, weather, entertainment, shopping and stock quotes) as well as its location by organizing them the way he/she chooses [**Yahoo**]. States and cities (restricted to the US) may be selected to get information on local weather, daily horoscopes can be obtained based on the birth date entered, and the user can choose from a wide variety of subjects like entertainment, home and family, health, music, business, computers and technology, personal finance, shopping, sports and outdoors, travel etc.

### 2.6.3. Your Store at amazon.com

The popular online book store Amazon.com is a highly diversified shopping portal with products and services covering books, apparel, sporting goods, music, DVDs, magazine subscriptions, videos, electronics goods, office products, software, medical and scientific supplies, home and garden items, car parts and accessories, kids' and baby items and gifts. A user can personalize this online store by indicating his/her interests. Creating a new account requires no credit card or personal information until one decides to purchase a product [**Amazon**]. A user can thus create a site login providing a specialized view of recommendations, new releases, best bargains etc.

## 2.7. LIBRARY PERSONALIZATION PROJECTS

In the context of libraries, through personalization, users start with a generic library and by making selections and choices create a personal library with pre-selected and relevant e-journals, databases, reference works, websites and other information resources. Also, they can view the different services offered by the library through a single window implementation strategy (there may be different systems for in-house resources and network accessed information, however, they appear as a single system to the user using the facilities) with provision for configuring alerts and automatic updates, enabling users to add/ remove resources of their choice. Since many projects have been undertaken by different libraries, only a few important ones are listed as an illustration to reflect what is possible and what is not.

### 2.7.1. MyLibrary @ Notre Dame University, USA

MyLibrary allows patrons to personalize and customize their view of the Libraries' website by cultivating more person-to-person relationships between patrons and librarians. To resolve the issues raised by users, it operates on the perception that information is hard to find and hard to get; and communication (between library and users in both ways) can be improved. To achieve this goal, it adopts a three-pronged strategy. First, subject specialist librarians create short lists of information resources pertinent to their clientele, and selected items from these lists are recommended over other items based on their importance to the subject area. Second, users visiting the libraries' websites are presented with a homogeneous set of information resources organized by title, subject area, popularity, recommendation, ease-of-use etc. Third, visitors are provided the option to create a MyLibrary account by submitting their name and email address, and to select a subject from a list of subject areas supported by the University (**Morgan**, 2002).

A software for creating a personalized library environment has been developed at Notre Dame University, enabling users to customize a "generic page" using a pick list of selected resources, and add personal links. As the librarian sends both global and subject discipline messages, users update their personal libraries as and when new resources are added. This software is used by several other universities such as NCSU, Auburn, Notre Dame, Lund, The Open University etc.

### 2.7.2. Mylibrary @ North Carolina State University, USA

MyLibrary is a user-driven, customizable information service that allows users to create a portable Web page, listing the available information resources by providing a little information about him/her [**MyLibrary@NCState**]. Technically, MyLibrary uses a relational database, a Web server and a set of scripts for providing mediation between the two. The database supporting MyLibrary contains links to information-rich content including full-text databases, data sets, bibliographic databases, electronic texts of all kinds, ready reference materials and most importantly, direct access to librarians. It is platform independent, can be accessed using a Web browser and is portable with users able to login to the service from any location. Because MyLibrary is easy to maintain, its content is continually kept up-to-date with dynamic global as well as discipline-specific messages. Options provided include 'Ask a Librarian', borrowing record, library catalogue, ILL/DDS request, suggest a purchase, University website links, quick searches on library catalogue and online dictionary/encyclopedia/Internet (Google), reference shelf (virtual reference collection), indexes and abstracts, electronic journals etc.

### 2.7.3. BUILDER at University of Birmingham, UK

The **BUILDER** Hybrid Library Demonstrator aims to demonstrate 'seamlessness', where all resources are accessible through the same interface and 'profiling', where the resources offered are relevant to individual user needs. This profile based personalization service encompasses course related materials, searches for information in University library catalogues in the West Midlands region, provides interactive guides for help, training and support, and offers a-z in services (representing the full list of products and services available). These include books, printed and electronic journals, web pages, conference proceedings, abstracts and indexes, databases, previous years' exam papers in electronic form (which might contain copyrighted material like extracts from books and music scores ; hence access is restricted to members of the University for the purpose of preparing for examinations), electronic reading list materials (book chapters and journal articles), encyclopedias and dictionaries, library catalogues, subject-specific gateways etc.

### 2.7.4. MyOpenLibrary Project at Open University, UK

The MyOpenLibrary Project attempts to deliver a personalized digital library environment to support the teaching and learning needs of students and staff, keeping in view the steady increase in the number of available resources and services as well as user constraints in navigating multiple information sources [**Myopenlibrary**]. The MyOpenLibrary system integrates itself with other existing Library technologies and systems like Voyager Library Management System, OU authentication systems, the web based ROUTES Internet resources database, the proposed 24 hour electronic helpdesk system OPAL and Endnote, a tool for managing bibliographic references. The project is conceived as a seamlessly integrated, user-focused interface for users to access their personal selection of library resources with linkages to other departmental and University-wide information systems offering on-line training and development activities. It also offers 24 hour advice and support, search tools/saved database searches, a personal library of resources, portable book marking tools, customized information packages of relevant resources, personalized email alerts to new resources based upon areas of interest and collaborative resources area (web conferencing, live chat and interactive web support). It further provides users the option of creating their own suite of library resources, stored links and bookmarks, saved searches, personalized email alerts of relevant resources and on-line training and development activities.

### 2.7.5. MyLibrary @ Los Alamos National Laboratory

The MyLibrary @LANL service allows users to collect and organize general web resources or other selected information contained at the Library's website. This service allows for individualized spaces and enhanced content besides ensuring that the users utilize only reliable and pertinent web data. MyLibrary provides users the opportunity to create and populate personalized Web environments called libraries. A personal library holds categories or divisions called folders; folders hold a collection of links. The MyLibrary @LANL organization is similar to the directory structure of systems, with libraries as directories, folders as sub-directories and Web links as files possessing the characteristics of bookmarks with the added features of quality, updation and flexibility (**Giacomo** *et al.*).

### 2.7.6. Other MyLibrary Projects

Other MyLibrary projects to personalize contents are currently operational at the libraries of Cornell University (**Cohen** *et al.*, 2000) and Virginia Commonwealth University (**Graphery**, 2002). As the use of digital libraries increases, users expect more than simply being able to filter, retrieve and refer to library materials, preferring instead to gain personalized access to library materials according to their personal requirements and interests [**Hiroshima University**].

### 2.7.7. NewsAgent for Libraries

NewsAgent for Libraries, one of the projects funded by the Electronic Libraries Programme (eLib) in the UK (URLs: http://newsagent.ukoln.ac.uk, http://www.sbu.ac.uk/ litc/ newsagent/) aims to create for library and information professionals a user configurable electronic news and current awareness service characterized by a mixture of content streams including metadata. Users' interests are specified by profiles which are then matched with incoming records so that users are automatically alerted by electronic mail of items of potential interest (**Tedd** and **Yeates**, 1998).

### 2.7.8. Personal Digital Library

The Personal Digital Library (PDL) under the ELINOR: Electronic Library Project at De Montfort University, Leicester, UK, attempts to develop a personal information system which acts as a front end to other electronic library systems and manages users' total information requirements. The PDL is designed to include the characteristics of adaptive contents whereby users have their own personal and personalized databases; support for interactive information retrieval by browsing and organizing search terms hierarchically; adaptive style with a customizable look and feel; and scalability so that users can build up their own personal collections (**Zhao**, 1998).

### 2.7.9. Headline

UK's Hybrid Electronic Access and Delivery in the Library Networked Environment (Headline) (URL: http://www.headline.ac.uk/) [**Headline**] project under the Electronic Libraries (eLib) programme explores possibilities of providing personalized content to its users.

### 2.7.10. Digital Portfolio Archives

The 'Digital Portfolio Archives' (DPAs) project at the University of California at Los Angeles concentrates on developing process models that transform primary sources into digital library content; allow teachers to build a personalized information system or DPAs containing the content and descriptions; and enable students to incorporate components of the teachers' DPA and additional project-related materials into their own DPAs. It also facilitates the optional incorporation of these DPAs back into the digital library, but as a distinct layer of user-created content distinguished by provenance. Content for the base digital library will be drawn from the seven archival, manuscript and museum repositories at UCLA. This content will be digitized and then described using the emerging SGML standard for both Encoded Archival Description and teacher annotations, and finally incorporated into a prototypical digital library structure. This process model will thereafter be applied in case studies relating to health and natural science education at the UCLA laboratory elementary school. The development and testing of the DPA process model builds on the work of, and feeds into, several educational projects underway at UCLA. These include innovative, cross-disciplinary collaborations with the Smithsonian Institutions, Los Angeles County Museum, and the University Research Library (**Gilliland-Swetland**, 1997).

## 2.8. RESEARCH IN THE INDIAN PERSPECTIVE

**Baradol** (1989) made a study of Current Awareness Services in Science libraries in the country, while **Vyasamurthy** (1990) conducted a study on design and development of a software package for microcomputer-based Information Retrieval and SDI. However, both studies were conducted before the advent of full text electronic databases and primary resources. Further studies were undertaken on various aspects of indexing and subject retrieval (**Bhattacharya**, 1980), (**Iyer**, 1984), (**Kamal**, 1984), (**Chattopadhyay**, 1993), and (**Areti**, 1995). **Devadasan** (1994) attempted to study computer based indexes for subject indexing. There have been other attempts to study and develop Information System Designs for different types of libraries or different subject specializations (**Murthy**, 1983), (**Singh**, 1994), and (**Goswami**, 1995). **Savanur** (1990) attempted content analysis approach for reviewing library science books, while **Sinha** (1989) made a critical study of scientific and technological services for industrial innovations. **Goriya** (1999) observed the problems and prospects of bibliographic database management system in the country. **Parameswaran** (1991) investigated the factors influencing the information services of a university library with special reference to Kerala University. **Dubey** (1984) designed a computerized decision system for managing resource sharing networks.

**Koganurmuth** (1975) assessed communication patterns and information seeking behavior among REC faculties. Another study attempted to examine resource sharing in scientific and technical libraries of the country (**Singh**, 1998). **Prakash** (1998) carried out an evaluative study on the design and development of bibliographic databases for engineering sciences. **Gupta** (1987) attempted to study collection management in professional college libraries. **Sangayya** (1997) explored the degree of job satisfaction among professionals in engineering and technology libraries in Karnataka. **Sridhar** (1989) examined the information seeking behavior of space technologists with an emphasis on correlating user characteristics with search behavior. **Jain** (1996) assessed scientists' use of periodicals in Physics, Chemistry and Botany in large-sized science and technology libraries in Delhi.

A few studies were also conducted on the various aspects

of IIT libraries. **Saibaba** (1992) carried out a study of co-operation and networking among engineering and technological libraries with special reference to the Indian Institutes of Technology. **Singh** (1985) studied professional attitudes of technical library personnel with special reference to the IITs. **Rao** (1993) studied the resources, services and uses of IIT libraries besides examining options for setting up a comprehensive library and information network. **Singh, S P** made an evaluative study of growth, development and services provided by IIT Libraries. However, despite these efforts, no concrete attempts have been made in our country so far to design an effective and workable library content personalization system.

## 2.9. CONCLUSION

The different personalization strategies discussed so far concentrate on utilizing various information technology tools to connect the resources at a personal level for maximum user convenience and optimal resource usage. Advancements in web enabled computing and continued user interest to gather information resources on the web forced many popular portals to bring in the concept of content personalization to suit appropriate user interests. Apart from selecting content, some services also provide options to select background colours, fonts, order of menus etc. In the case of libraries, users start with a generic library and by making selections and choices create a personal library with pre-selected and relevant information resources. Also, the user can view the different services offered by the library through a single interface providing links to different services and resources in multiple servers inside and outside the library. Library personalization projects are operational at Notre Dame University, North Carolina State University Los Alamos National Laboratory, Cornell University, Virginia Commonwealth University and University of California, Los Angeles (all USA), University of Birmingham, Open University, De Montfort University, Leicester (all UK), apart from special projects like NewsAgent for Libraries and Hybrid

Electronic Access and Delivery in the Library Networked Environment (Headline) in UK.

However, no concrete attempts have been made in our country so far to design an effective and workable library personalization system. Thus it is evident that a sizeable gap exists in implementing personalization activities in our libraries in the manner adopted by personalized library projects abroad, through employing the tools and techniques mentioned. Personalization needs a good collection of electronic resources as well as sufficient number of serious users, both of which are easily available in many of our libraries. Further, libraries with considerable experience in providing electronic information services should explore the possibility of a pragmatic extension of personalization techniques to Indian libraries. In the next chapter, libraries of IITs are examined to explore the possibilities of implementing library personalization in the Indian context.

## REFERENCES

1. **Amazon**, http://www.amazon.com
2. **Andonyadis** (Christo George). A hybrid architecture for Web-based personal healthcare support agents. The George Washington University. D. Sc. 2000. 184 p.
3. **Areti** (R P). Application of Computer Based Natural Language Processing Tools and Techniques in Developing Subject Indexing Languages. Karnatak University. Ph. D. 1995.
4. **Armengol** (E) and **Plaza** (E). Explanation-based learning: a knowledge level analysis. *Artificial Intelligence Review*. 9, 1; Feb 1995; 19-35.
5. **Asthana** (A) and **Krzyzanowski** (P). A small domain communications system for personalized shopping assistance. *International Conference on Personal Wireless Communications*. 1994. IEEE. 1994. p 199 – 203.
6. **Baradol** (A K). Current Awareness Services in Science Libraries in India. Karnatak University. Ph. D. 1989.

7. **Bhattacharya** (G). General Theory of Subject Indexing Language. Karnatak University. Ph. D. 1980.

8. **Bianchi-Berthouze** (N) and **Kato** (T). Querying and personalizing the Web: a multimedia personal assistant. *International Conference on Systems, Man, and Cybernetics*. 2000. IEEE. 2000. V 1. p 678 – 683.

9. **Bogonikolos** (N) *et al.*. "ARCHIMIDES": an intelligent agent for adaptive-personalized navigation within a WEB server. *International Conference on System Sciences* (HICSS-32), 32nd, Hawaii, 1999. 9 p.

10. **Bradley (P).** Personalised news services: how personal, how much news?. *Information World Review*. 152; Nov 1999; 47-48.

11. **Builder**, http://www.builder.bham.ac.uk/hld/passportmenu.asp

12. **Cao** (Fang). An integrated overview of key issues in data mining. Daltech-Dalhousie University (Canada). MCompSc. 1998. 105 p.

13. **Carchiolo (V)** *et al.*. Courses personalization in an e-learning environment. *International Conference on Advanced Learning Technologies*, 3rd, 2003. IEEE. p 252 – 253.

14. **Chattopadhyay** (A). Role of Subject Indexing Languages on the Design and Development of Online Bibliographic Information Storage and Retrieval System. Jadavpur University. Ph. D. 1993.

15. **Chen** (Andrew Nai-Kuang). Improving database performances in a changing environment with uncertain and dynamic information demand: An intelligent database system approach. The University of Connecticut. Ph. D. 1999. 195 p.

16. **Cheong** (S N) *et al.*. A web-based collaborative enabled multimedia content authoring and management system for interactive and personalized online learning. *International*

*Conference on Computers in Education*, 2002. V2. p 872 – 873.

17. **Cohen** (Suzanne) *et al.* MyLibrary: Personalized Electronic Services in the Cornell University Library. *D-Lib Magazine*. 6, 4; April 2000. http://www.dlib.org/dlib/april00/mistlebauer/04mistlebauer.html

18. **Cosinger** (A) *et al.* AI meets Authoring User Models for Intelligent Multimedia. *Artificial Intelligence Review*. 8, 5-6; 1994-95; 447-68.

19. **Dadarlat** (V) *et al.* A personalized approach for teaching Web-based curriculum in Communications & Computer Networks. *Canadian Conference on Electrical and Computer Engineering*, (IEEE CCECE 2002), 2002. V2. p 732 – 737.

20. **Dahn** (I) and **Schwabe** (G). Personalizing textbooks with slicing technologies - concept, tools, architecture, collaborative use. *International Conference on System Sciences* (HICSS), 35th, Hawaii, 2002. 10 p.

21. **Devadasan** (F J). Computer Based System for Generating Types of Subject Index and Alphabetical Thesaurus Based on the Structure of Subject Indexing Languages. Karnatak University. Ph. D. 1994.

22. **Dubey** (Y P). Computerised decision system for management of resource sharing network. University of Pittsburgh. Ph. D. 1984.

23. **Futrelle** (R P) and **Smith** (Linda C). Expert systems using semantic representations of full text for question answering. *Information interaction: Annual Meeting*, 45th, Columbus, Ohio, 17-21 October 1982, ASIS. Petrarca (A E). *et al. Ed*, White Plains, New York, Knowledge Industry Publications, 1982. V19. p 103-106.

24. **Giacomo** (Mariella Di) *et al.* MyLibrary, A Personalization Service for Digital Library Environments. http://www.ercim.org/publication/ws-proceedings/DelNoe02/

Giacomo.pdf

25. **Gilliland-Swetland** (A). The Digital Portfolio Archives project. California University at Los Angeles. Department of Library and Information Science, Current 1997.

26. **Goriya** (Sunil). Bibliographic Database Management System in India: Problems and Prospects. Vikram University. Ph. D. 1999.

27. **Goswami** (P R). Statistical Information System in India: A Proposed Model. Delhi, University. Ph. D. 1995.

28. **Gupta** (S R). Management of Library Collections of Professional Colleges in India. BHU. Ph. D. 1987.

29. **Ha** (Sung Ho). Helping online customers decide through Web personalization. *IEEE Intelligent Systems*. 17, 6; Nov.-Dec. 2002; 34 – 43.

30. **Hawryszkiewycz** (I T). Agent support for personalized learning services. *International Conference on Advanced Learning Technologies*, 3rd, 2003. IEEE. p 332 - 333.

31. **Headline,** http://www.headline.ac.uk/public/diss/jp-PIE-HybLib-model/

32. **Hicks** (D). Towards support for personalization and customization in a collaborative environment, *International Conference on Computer Supported Cooperative Work in Design*, 7th, 2002. IEEE. p 336 – 341.

33. **Hiroshima University,** http://www.isl.hiroshima-u.ac.jp/html/digital_library.html

34. **Hsu** (Hui-Huang) *et al.* Towards error-free and personalized Web-based courses, *International Conference on Advanced Information Networking and Applications*, (AINA 2003), 17th, 2003. p 99 – 104.

35. **Iyer** (Hemalatha). Structure of Indexing Language and Retrieval Effectiveness. Mysore University. Ph. D. 1984.

**36.** **Jain** (R) and **Anjum** (F). Mobile agents for personalized information retrieval: when are they a good idea?, *Wireless Communications and Networking Conference*, (2000 WCNC), 2000. IEEE. V1. p 242 – 245.

**37.** **Jain** (Sarita). Use of Periodicals in Physics, Chemistry, and Botany by scientists in large-size science and technology libraries in Delhi. Delhi University. Ph. D. 1996.

**38.** **Johnson** (A) and **Fotouhi** (F). Adaptive indexing in very large databases. *Journal of Database Management*. 6, 1; Winter 1995; 4-12.

**39.** **Johnson** (A) and **Fotouhi** (F). Adaptive clustering of hypermedia documents. *Information Systems*. 21, 6; September 1996; 459-73.

**40.** **Jones** (Richard L) and **Corbett** (Dan). Automatic document content analysis: the AIDA project. *Library Hi Tech*. 10, 1-2; 1992; 111-117.

**41.** **Kamal** (Awad Atef). Optimum Algorithms in Subject Indexing System. Delhi University. Ph. D. 1984.

**42.** **Kantamneni** (R G Prasad) and **Narayanan** (S). Personalization of information retrieval through user profiling. *International Conference on Systems, Man, and Cybernetics*, 2001. IEEE. V5. p 3475 – 3478.

**43.** **Karagiannidis** (C) *et al.* An architecture for defining re-usable adaptive educational content. *International Conference on Advanced Learning Technologies*, 2001. IEEE. p 21 – 24.

**44.** **Kavanagh** (Judith). The Text Analyzer: A tool for knowledge acquisition from texts. University of Ottawa (Canada). MCSc. 1995. 138 p.

**45.** **Kim** (Jin Baek) *et al.* A framework for dynamic eBusiness negotiation processes. *International Conference on E-Commerce*, (CEC 2003), 2003. IEEE. p 84 – 91.

46. **Kim** (Kibum) *et al.* An empirical study of Web personalization assistants supporting end-users in Web information systems. *Symposia on Human Centric Computing Languages and Environments*, 2002. IEEE. p 60 – 62.

47. **Koganurmuth** (M M). Communication Pattern and Information Seeking Behaviours among the Teaching Faculties of REC in India. Karnatak University. Ph. D. 1975.

48. **Koyama** (A) *et al.* An agent-based personalized distance learning system. *International Conference on Information Networking*, 15th, 2001. p 895 – 899.

49. **Li** (Xuhong). Automatic Document Classification and Extraction System (ADoCES). New Jersey Institute of Technology. Ph. D. 1999. 147 p.

50. **Liu** (Duen-Ren) *et al.* A framework for personalized e-catalogs: an integration of XML-based metadata, user models and agents. *International Conference on System Sciences*, (HICSS), 34th, Hawaii, 2001. 10 p.

51. **Maarek** (Y S) and **Shaul** (I Z B). Automatically organizing bookmarks per contents. *Computer Networks and ISDN Systems*. 28, 7-11; 1996; 1321-33.

52. **Matthijssen** (L). A task-based interface to legal databases. *Artificial Intelligence and Law*. 6, 1; 1998; 81-103.

53. **McKeown** *et al.* Leveraging a common representation for personalized search and summarization in a medical digital library. *Joint Conference on Digital Libraries*, 2003. p. 159 – 170.

54. **Miao** (Chunyan) *et al.* Fuzzy cognitive agents for personalized recommendation. *International Conference on Web Information Systems Engineering*, (WISE 2002), 3rd, 12-14 Dec. 2002. p 362 – 371.

55. **Miettinen** (M). *et al.* EDUCOSM - personalized writable

Web for learning communities. *International Conference on Information Technology: Coding and Computing [Computers and Communications]*, (ITCC 2003), 2003. p 37 – 42.

56. **Morgan** (Eric Lease). Making Information Easier to Find With MyLibrary. http://www.nd.edu/~ladvance/access/issues/2002/Fall/MyLibrary.htm

57. **Murthy** (T A V). Design and Development of an Information System for Small Industry. Karnatak University. Ph. D. 1983.

58. **MyLibrary@NCState,** http://my.lib.ncsu.edu/

59. **Myopenlibrary,** http://library.open.ac.uk/aboutus/myolib/index.htm

60. **Narayanan** (S) *et al.* Design of model-based interfaces for a real world information system. *IEEE Transactions on Systems, Man and Cybernetics*, Part A. 32, 1; Jan. 2002; 11 – 24.

61. **Niu** (Li) *et al.* Product hierarchy-based customer profiles for electronic commerce recommendation. *International Conference on Machine Learning and Cybernetics*, 2002. V2. p 1075 – 1080.

62. **Oehlmann** (R). Evaluating a case-based discovery system: a case-study in content-oriented Evaluation. *Artificial Intelligence in Medicine*. 12, 1; Jan 1998; 61-76.

63. **O'Leary** (D E). Using AI in knowledge management: knowledge bases and ontologies. *IEEE Intelligent Systems*. 13, 3; May/Jun 1998; 34-9.

64. **Panteleyev** (M G) *et al.* Intelligent educational environments based on the semantic Web technologies. *International Conference on Artificial Intelligence Systems*, (ICAIS 2002), 2002. IEEE. p 457 – 462.

65. **Papanikolaou** (K A) and **Grigoriadou** (M). An instructional framework supporting personalized learning

on the Web. *International Conference on Advanced Learning Technologies*, 3rd, 2003. IEEE. p 120 – 124.

66. **Parameswaran** (N). An Investigation into the factors that influence the information services of a university library with special reference to Kerala University. Cochin University. Ph. D. 1991.

67. **Prakash** (T N). Design and Development of Bibliographic Database for Engineering Sciences: An Evaluative Study. Bangalore University. Ph. D. 1998.

68. **Qu** (Hong-Ting) and **Shen** (Rui-Min). The design and implementation of personalized learning navigation system. *International Conference on Machine Learning and Cybernetics*. 2002. V3. p 1310 – 1313.

69. **Quarati** (A). Designing shareable and personalisable e-learning paths. *International Conference on Information Technology: Coding and Computing [Computers and Communications]*, (ITCC 2003), 2003. p 454 – 460.

70. **Rao** (Pilla Bhaskara). The IIT Libraries: A Study of their Resources, Services and Uses with a Proposal for Setting up of a Library & Information Network. Andhra University. Ph. D. 1993.

71. **Rediff**, http://www.rediff.com/cms/registration.jsp

72. **Saibaba** (B). A Study of Co-operation and Technological Networking among Engineering and Technological Libraries in India with special reference to Indian Institute of Technology. Burdwan University. Ph. D. 1992.

73. **Sangayya** (S Sirur). Job Satisfaction among the Professionals working in the Engineering and Technology Libraries in Karnataka: A Study. Bangalore University. Ph. D. 1997.

74. **Savanur** (S K). Reviewing of Library Science Books: A Content Analysis Approach. Karnatak University. Ph. D. 1990.

**75.** **Savoy** (J). Searching information in legal hypertext systems. *Artificial Intelligence and Law*. 2, 3; 1993-1994; 205-32.

**76.** **Schraefel** (M C) *et al.* Building virtual communities for research collaboration. *Academia/Industry Working Conference on Research Challenges*, 2000. IEEE. p 27 – 32.

**77.** **Schubert** (P). The pivotal role of community building in electronic commerce, *International Conference on System Sciences*, 33rd, Hawaii, 2000. IEEE. V1. 8 p.

**78.** **Schuegraf** (E J) and **Bommel** (F V). An automatic document indexing system based on cooperating expert systems: design and development. *Canadian Journal of Information and Library Science*. 18, 2; Jul 93; 32-50.

**79.** **Shibata** (H) *et al.* Agent technology recommending personalized information and its evaluation. *International Workshop on Autonomous Decentralized System*, 2nd, 2002. p 176 – 183.

**80.** **Shukla** (K K). Some AI techniques for information retrieval. *DESIDOC Bulletin of Information Technology*. 16, 4; Jul 96; 13-18.

**81.** **Singh** (B N). Professional Attitude of Library Personnel of Technical Libraries in India with special reference to IITs. BHU. Ph.D. 1985.

**82.** **Singh** (Gurudav). Resource Sharing in Scientific and Technical Libraries in India: A Study. Jammu University. Ph. D. 1998.

**83.** **Singh** (Jai Prakash). Development of a Model Information Retrieval System for Laser Technology. Delhi University. Ph. D. 1994.

**84.** **Singh (S P)**. IIT Libraries in India: An Evaluative Study of their Growth Development and Services. Delhi University. Ph. D.

85. **Sinha** (A K). Scientific and Technological Services for Industrial Innovations: A Critical Study of Indian Situation. Rajasthan University. Ph. D. 1989.

86. **Sridhar** (M S). Information seeking behaviour of space technologists with emphasis on correlating user's characteristics with search behaviour, Mysore University. Ph. D. 1989.

87. **Tang** (Changjie) *et al.* Personalized courseware construction based on Web data mining. International Conference on Web Information Systems Engineering, 2000. V2. p. 204 – 211.

88. **Tedd** (L A) and **Yeates** (R). A personalised current awareness service for library and information services staff: an overview of the NewsAgent for Libraries project. Program. 32, 4; Oct 1998; 373-90.

89. **Vyasamurthy** (P). Design and Development of Software Package for Information Retrieval and SDI using Micro Computer. Gulbarga University. Ph. D. 1990.

90. **Wellman** (M P) *et al.* The digital library as a community of information agents. *IEEE Expert*. 11, 3; Jun 96; 10-11.

91. **Wu** (Hong). Choice of techniques in data mining: Three experiments in applications. The American University. MS. 1999. 50 p.

92. **Wu** (Kun-Lung) *et al.* Personalization with Dynamic Profiler, *International Workshop on Advanced Issues of E-Commerce and Web-Based Information Systems*, WECWIS 2001, 3rd, 2001. p 12 – 20.

93. **Xiao** (Li) *et al.* The tuneup and integration of resources in Web-based learning, *International Conference on Advanced Learning Technologies*, 2001. IEEE. p 391 – 394.

94. **Xingshe** (Zhou) *et al.* A multi-agent system for personalized and private service in PDR. *International*

*Conference on Information Technology: Coding and Computing [Computers and Communications]*, (ITCC 2003), 2003. p 635-639.

95. **Yahoo**, http://my.yahoo.com/?myHome

96. **Youm** (Sun-Hee) and **Cho** (Dong-Sub). Personalized recommendation based on item dependency map. *International Symposium on Industrial Electronics*, (ISIE 2001), 2001. IEEE. V1. p 250 - 253.

97. **Yu** (Kai) *et al.* Probabilistic memory-based collaborative filtering. *IEEE Transactions on Knowledge and Data Engineering*. 16, 1; Jan. 2004; 56 – 69.

98. **Yu** (P S). Data mining and personalization technologies. *International Conference on Database Systems for Advanced Applications*, 6th, 1999. p 6 – 13.

99. **Zarri** (G P). A rule-based approach to the semantic parsing of natural language documents. *International Journal of Applied Expert Systems*. 2, 1; 1994; 39-53.

100. **Zhang** (G) *et al.* Research on Web education system with personalized navigations. *International Conference on Advanced Information Networking and Applications*, (AINA 2004), 18th, 2004. V1. p 451 – 456.

101. **Zhao** (D). The Personal Digital Library. *In* ELINOR: Electronic Library Project. London: Bowker-Saur for British Library. 1998. p 97-103.

102. **Zhu** (B) *et al.* Creating a large-scale digital library for georeferenced information. *D-Lib Magazine*. 5, 7/8; Jul/Aug 1999. http://www.dlib.org/dlib/july99/zhu/07zhu.html

## Chapter 3
# Personalization Model For IIT Libraries

### 3.0. INTRODUCTION

The personalization attempts discussed in the previous chapter give us an idea of the different personalization options, techniques and tools applicable in various service contexts in general and libraries in particular. In the backdrop of this experience and vital knowledge, a questionnaire was prepared to assess both the state of the art technology in the Indian libraries by focusing on the different IIT libraries as well as their level of preparedness to initiate personalization services. Library & Information Science, falling within the purview of social science, necessitates a research study on libraries to judge the present status, on the basis of which their future can be predicted. The current study is experimental in its scope to explore personalized service in digitized form for electronic resources in libraries of higher educational institutes of world class standards like the IITs. But a questionnaire method has also been attempted for two reasons: first, to assess the preparedness of these libraries to venture into such client centred state of the art services, and second, to test the validity of extrapolating the personalization system currently under development at Central Library, IIT Kharagpur as a model to other IITs.

A questionnaire (Annexure 1) was prepared and sent in December 2001 to the Librarians of all the seven IITs to assess the present status of their collection, services, computer infrastructure, electronic information facilities and services, and to judge their awareness of personalization as also their opinion regarding initiating the same. The respondents were also asked to provide information regarding the present availability of and any future plans for providing personalization services in their libraries. In addition, study visits to assess and observe the facilities were also undertaken to IIT Bombay and IIT Madras to compare their respective facilities with those available in IIT Kharagpur. The questionnaires administered to IIT Madras and IIT Kanpur were not returned despite repeated reminders. An attempt was then made to collect every possible information regarding these Institutes from their official websites or other available sources like annual reports, institute publications etc. The aggregate percentage of response being above 70%, which can be taken as reliable data for generalization purpose. Since the IITs are coordinated at the national level by the IIT Council with Directors of the individual Institutes as its members, the Institutes have similar academic and teaching programmes. As the IITs have largely identical teaching, research, and library and information support facilities, lack of response from two of the Institutes does not significantly affect the findings of this study.

Tabular presentation of data being more pleasing to the eye than mere description of facts, data collected in the study has been presented in a number of tables wherever required. Personalization is a relatively new concept applicable only in libraries with proficient manpower, information hungry clientele and sufficient electronic content; hence the questions asked cover a wide range of areas like infrastructure, resources, services, staff, budget etc. Tables 3.1 to 3.12 deal with general details regarding the libraries, their collections, electronic resources, budget, staff and computer infrastructure. Tables 3.13 to 3.16 discuss the different electronic information services currently offered by these libraries. Table 3.17 covers details about users and profiling, both of which are extremely significant in the context of personalization. Tables 3.18 and 3.19 highlight various aspects of content personalization. The results of the analysis confirm the utility of taking the library of one of the IITs as a model for conducting the study.

## 3.1. Book Collection in IIT Libraries

*Table 3.1: Book Collection in IIT Libraries*

| *Institution* | *Name of Library* | *Year of Establishment* | *Code used in the Study* | *No. of Books* |
|---|---|---|---|---|
| Indian Institute of Technology Bombay, Mumbai | Central Library | 1958 | MUM | 2,07,370 |
| Indian Institute of Technology Delhi, Delhi | Central Library | 1962 | DLH | 1,68,373 |
| Indian Institute of Technology Gauhati, Gauhati | Central Library | 1995 | GHT | 30,000 |
| Indian Institute of Technology Kanpur, Kanpur | P K Kelkar Library | 1959 | KNP | 2,09,581 |
| Indian Institute of Technology, Kharagpur | Central Library | 1951 | KGP | 2,11,049 |
| Indian Institute of Technology Madras, Chennai | Central Library | 1959 | CHN | 3,47,975 (include bound journals & items in Table 3.3) |
| Indian Institute of Technology Roorkee, Roorkee | Central Library | 1847 (as an IIT in 2001) | RKE | 2,65,421 |

The questionnaire used in the study asked the respondents details like the name of the Institution and its library with year of establishment and the strength of the book collection. These questions were incorporated to essentially highlight the growth of these Institutions over the years in terms of collection. Table 3.1 presents the name of the Institute and Library, year of establishment, three letter codes used in the study to designate the different IIT libraries and the strength of their respective book collections. The Central Library of IIT Kharagpur emerges as the oldest, while all libraries other than that of IIT Gauhati hold a collection of over 2 lakhs. Gauhati is being provided with extra grants to upgrade its collection, having procured 30,000 books in just seven years of its existence. Roorkee is the oldest engineering educational institution in the country, holding a relatively large collection of books, though the IIT status was accorded to it very recently in 2001.

The IITs are special institutes meant for teaching and research in engineering and technology, with the sciences and humanities being used to support this core activity. However, since the science departments, like the engineering streams, offer courses and conduct research, the overall science collection is as strong as the engineering collection. These Institutes procure more specialized (and often costly) books meant for state of the art education and research in the applied sciences; hence their collections may not be as large in numbers as that of a University established during that period. However, as far as the quality of collection is concerned, they are undoubtedly the very best in the country and comparable with facilities in developed countries, considering the budget constraints they operate under and the overall status of engineering education in the country.

## 3.2. JOURNALS HOLDINGS

*Table 3.2: Journals Holdings*

| *Code* | *Current Journals* | | | *Bound Volumes* |
|---|---|---|---|---|
| | *Indian* | *Foreign* | *Total* | *of Journals* |
| MUM | 282 | 918 | 1190 | 95437 |
| DLH | | | 800 | 80000 |
| GHT | 200 | 550 | 750 | 20000 |
| KNP | | | 1200 | 135,000 |
| KGP | 150 | 950 | 1100 | 93652 |
| CHN | | | 890 | |
| RKE | 82 | 270 | 352 | |

Journals play an important role in the higher education and research scene, hence the questionnaire attempted to determine the strength of archival and current collection of journals in the various IIT Libraries. As far as content personalization is concerned, journals in electronic format emerge as the dominant mode of content used. Thus this question also compares the status of print journals with electronic journals. Table 3.2 highlights the total number of current journals being subscribed to by the different IIT Libraries as well as their collections of old journal volumes. As far as strength and quality is concerned, the journal collection in the IITs is rated as the best in the country. Though RKE has a good collection of books, its overall journal collection is not as strong as that of the other IIT Libraries, since its budget allocation outside the IIT stream permits only one third of the other IITs' subscription. This situation might have improved in recent years due to extra budget allocation and comparable status with other Institutes. KNP has the best collection of current as well as back volumes of journals with MUM and KGP coming next, followed by CHN, DLH and GHT.

## 3.3. NON-BOOK AND NON-PRINT SOURCES

*Table 3.3: Non-Book and Non-Print Sources*

| *Code* | *Standards, Patents etc.* | *Theses* | *Audio Cassettes* | *Video Cassettes* | *Micro-forms* | *Others* |
|---|---|---|---|---|---|---|
| MUM | 65,514 | 12,000 | 27 | 240 | 170 | |
| DLH | 26,923 | | | | | Reports-13430 |
| GHT | 400 | 50 | | 150 | | |
| KNP | 10,000 | 15,000 | | | 10,000 | Reports-25,000 |
| KGP | 8,024 | 2,485 | | 1268 | 2,000 | CDs-1310<br>Floppies-1800 |
| CHN | | | | 213 | | |
| RKE | | 1,500 | | | 10,000 | |

IIT libraries attach an equal importance to non-book sources as well since these are of prime significance to their teaching and research activities. These materials include standards, patents, theses, microforms, reports and non-print sources like audiocassettes, videocassettes, etc. Some of these sources are now available in electronic format, permitting them to be included as content for operating the personalization service. Table 3.3 summarizes the strength of non-book sources like standards, patents, theses, microforms and reports; and non-print sources like audiocassettes, videocassettes, CDs and floppies received with printed books in the different IIT Libraries. While the status of standards and patents from CHN and RKE is not available, that of MUM is very strong, followed closely by DLH, KNP and KGP. KGP does not keep B. Sc, B. Tech, M. Sc and M. Tech theses in its Central Library, and has a total of 2,485 Ph. D. theses. It also has a good collection of electronic supplements of printed books in CD and floppy format. MUM and KNP keep all theses and their number is over 10,000. KNP and DLH have an impressive collection of reports.

## 3.4. ELECTRONIC INFORMATION SOURCES

*Table 3.4: Electronic Information Sources*

| *Code* | *Electronic Journals (e-journals)* | | | *Electronic Books (e-books)* | | |
|---|---|---|---|---|---|---|
| | *CD* | *Web* | *Other* | *CD* | *Web/Intranet* | *Other* |
| MUM | 40 | 1600 | | 327 | 27 | |
| DLH | | 1400 | | | | |
| GHT | 20 | 200 | | 400 | | 2 |
| KGP | 100 | 600 | | | | |
| CHN | | 1260 | | | | |
| RKE | | 20 | | | | |

Data relating to electronic resources in the library helps assess the range of content available for personalization. Table 3.4 highlights the strength of electronic journals and electronic books in the different IIT libraries. MUM has more e-journals than other IITs, though DLH and CHN house over 1000 such journals. The number of e-journals listed in this table is the one accessible before the establishment of the Indian National Digital Library in Engineering Science and Technology (INDEST) consortium. Set up in 2003 under the Ministry of Human Resources Development (MHRD) for libraries in premier institutions, the INDEST consortium has made a significant improvement in the number of current as well as back issues of e-journals that can be currently accessed (**Arora** and **Agrawal**, 2003). As a result of this initiative, the number of full text e-journals in IIT Kharagpur has increased almost nine fold, from 600 journals in 2000 to 5381 journals in 2003. Since the various Institutes have common resources, INDEST has also enabled the personalization of electronic resources in different Institutes to be perceived as a single project. In the pre-INDEST era, different Institutes had access rights to different sets of resources; hence development of personalization services might have required development of multiple systems to cater to the diversity of resources accessed. Compared to electronic journals, books in electronic form are negligibly small. Only GHT and MUM responded to the question regarding the number of e-books. KGP houses a good collection of CDs and floppies which are received with printed books.

## 3.5. MEDIA AND TYPE OF ELECTRONIC DATABASES

*Table 3.5: Media and Type of Electronic Databases*

| *Code* | *Electronic Databases (Media)* | | | *Electronic Databases (Type)* | | |
|---|---|---|---|---|---|---|
| | *CD* | *Web* | *Others* | *Bibliographic* | *Full Text* | *Others* |
| MUM | 6 | | | 6 | | |
| DLH | 12 | | | | | |
| GHT | ✓ | | ✓ | ✓ | | |
| CHN | 7 | | | 7 | | |
| KNP | 11 | | | 6 | 5 | |
| KGP | 15 | | 5 | 14 | 6 | |
| RKE | | | | ✓ | | |

IIT libraries acquire electronic databases (bibliographic and full text) over a period of time in different media such as floppy and CD-ROM as well as those accessible through web. The onset of e-journals and their access through web enabled this media to emerge as the dominant mode for subscribing to e-resources. The present study attempted to tackle content accessed through web. Table 3.5 lists the details of electronic databases held by the different IIT Libraries. Right from making available bibliographic databases in CD-ROM format a decade back, the IIT Libraries have been housing a comprehensive collection of electronic databases in different disciplines and areas of specialization. They were also the very first institutes in the country to acquire full text databases (like IEEE/IEE Electronic Library) and standards. KGP has 15 CD databases followed by DLH with 12 and KNP with 11. In all the Institutes, the majority of databases available are bibliographic in nature, whereas KGP and KNP have many full text databases also. GHT and RKE have not indicated the exact number of electronic databases available with them.

## 3.6. PRINT VS ELECTRONIC PREFERENCE

*Table 3.6: Preferred Format for Acquiring Resources*

| *Code* | *Format Preference* | | | *Reasons* |
|---|---|---|---|---|
| | *Paper* | *Electronic* | *Microform* | |
| MUM | | ✓ | | Easily available on Intranet |
| GHT | ✓ | | | Reliable<br>Conventional<br>Comfortable for users |
| KGP | | ✓ | | Easy to handle and use<br>Better search features<br>Easy networking options<br>Preferred by a majority of users |
| RKE | ✓ | | | Readers are more comfortable with paper |

When an information resource is available in print as well as in electronic form, the preference expressed by the library staff and users reveals their level of technological awareness. The more technology friendly they are, the more receptive they will be to new technology-intrinsic services like content personalization. Table 3.6 presents details about the format preferred by different libraries for acquiring information resources. MUM and KGP preferred electronic form due to the distinct advantages of easy availability on Intranet, ease in handling and use, better search features, easy networking option and users' preference for electronic media. GHT and RKE opted for paper as the preferred medium due to obvious assets like reliability, conventional format and comfortable for readers. Regardless of the choices made, it is clear that there are two distinct categories of users in the IITs: old timers who still prefer everything in print, and newcomers who show a marked preference for electronic sources. In addition, there are a large number of users who are comfortable with both formats at different stages of the information use cycle. These users prefer the electronic format while searching because of its explicit advantages over print. However, after identifying the relevant sources they prefer reading them in print format due to easy handling and use in library, laboratory, classroom or home. They may again return to the electronic form while citing or quoting references in their papers. The above table clearly indicates the success and acceptance electronic information has received in these Institutes. Thus it may safely be concluded that the dominance and acceptance of electronic information will be even more visible in future.

## 3.7. ELECTRONIC JOURNALS

As highly valuable tools of teaching and research, electronic journals play a dominant role in the entire spectrum of electronic content available in the IIT libraries. The types of electronic journals mostly in use and the reasons for acquiring them reveals the comfort level of the library and its users with this sort of electronic content, a prerequisite for the practice of content personalization service. Table 3.7 depicts the types of e-journals found in different IIT Libraries and reasons for acquiring them. All the respondents have abstracting and indexing as well as full text e-journals whereas MUM, GHT and KGP house back volumes of e-journals too. Common reasons for acquiring e-journals include minimizing of problems of theft and mutilation, ease of maintenance, networking facility and solving the space problem. In the case of RKE, additional reasons include free availability with print material and saving of readers' time while for KGP these include convenience in search and use, user preference and free availability with print subscription.

*Table 3.7: Types of e-journals and reasons for acquiring*

| Code | Types of e-journals | | | Reasons for Acquiring e-journals [1-Economic, 2-Solve problems of theft and mutilation, 3-Easy to maintain, 4-Provide networking facility, 5-Solve space problem, 6-Any other] | | | | | |
|---|---|---|---|---|---|---|---|---|---|
| | Indexing & Abstracting | Full Text | | | | | | | |
| | | Current Issues | Back Volumes | 1 | 2 | 3 | 4 | 5 | 6 |
| MUM | ✓ | ✓ | ✓ | | | | | | |
| DLH | ✓ | ✓ | | | | | | | |
| GHT | ✓ | ✓ | ✓ | | | ✓ | ✓ | ✓ | |
| KGP | ✓ | ✓ | ✓ | | ✓ | ✓ | ✓ | ✓ | Convenient to search and use |
| | | | | | | | | | User preference |
| | | | | | | | | | Free with print subscription |
| RKE | ✓ | ✓ | | | | | | | Available free with print |
| | | | | | | | | | Saves readers' time |

## 3.8. BUDGET FOR BOOKS AND JOURNALS

*Table 3.8: Budget for Books and Journals*

| Code | 1998-1999 | | | 1999-2000 | | | 2000-2001 | | |
|---|---|---|---|---|---|---|---|---|---|
| | Books (Lakhs) | Journals (Crores) | Total (Crores) | Books (Lakhs) | Journals (Crores) | Total (Crores) | Books (Lakhs) | Journals (Crores) | Total (Crores) |
| MUM | 32 | 2.16 | 2.48 | 32 | 2.47 | 2.79 | 32 | 2.51 | 2.83 |
| DLH | | | | 20 | 2.56 | 3.56 | | | |
| GHT | 448 | 1.20 | 5.68 | 128 | 1.30 | 2.58 | 324 | 1.76 | 5.00 |
| KNP | | | | | | | 60 | 5.00 | 5.79 |
| KGP | 28 | 2.69 | 2.97 | 50 | 3.16 | 3.66 | 46 | 3.94 | 4.40 |
| RKE | | | | | | | | 0.75 | 1.16 |

The amount spent annually on books and journals reflects the libraries' interest in significantly meeting their clients' information needs. The budget spent on these dominant categories also hints at the allocation for electronic resources and IT infrastructure, both of which are important to personalization activities. Table 3.8 provides details of the budget for procuring books and journals in IIT libraries. KNP's budget for books and journals exceeds that of KGP and MUM, whereas GHT invests more than five times than KNP for books, possibly for building up the essential collection expected in an IIT. RKE has a relatively smaller allocation for journals compared to other Institutes; however, this scenario might have changed, as in the case of the special grant for GHT, in later financial years. The journal budget shows a steady rise to match the corresponding price hike without dropping essential subscriptions due to the primary nature of information contained in them and their importance for research. However, this trend was not visible in the allocation for books.

## 3.9. BUDGET ALLOCATION

*Table 3.9: Budget Allocation and Feedback on Allocation for IT Related Products*

| ***Code*** | ***Budget Allocation to Different Heads*** | | ***Budget Spent on IT Related Products*** | | |
|---|---|---|---|---|---|
| | ***Fixed*** | ***Revised*** | ***More*** | ***Appropriate*** | ***Less*** |
| MUM | | ✓ | | | ✓ |
| GHT | | ✓ | | ✓ | |
| KGP | | ✓ | | ✓ | |
| RKE | | ✓ | | ✓ | |

Budget allocation for IT related products is of crucial significance to personalization service as a part of the allocation in this area would be utilized for setting up the desired infrastructure for personalization service. Table 3.9 displays the details regarding budget allocation in the different IIT libraries. Budget allocation to different heads in IIT libraries is not fixed but revised from time to time. GHT, KGP and RKE expressed the view that the amount spent on IT related products is appropriate while MUM is of the opinion that it should be increased.

### 3.10. STAFF

*Table 3.10: Staff*

| *Code* | *L* | *DL* | *AL* | *SA* | *STA* | *TA* | *Clerk* | *Attendant* | *Support* | *Others* | *Total* |
|---|---|---|---|---|---|---|---|---|---|---|---|
| MUM | 1 | 1 | 5 | | 10 | 2 | 7 | 14 | | 12 | 52 |
| DLH | | 3 | 1 | | 12 | 4 | 6 | 10 | | 1 | 37 |
| GHT | | 1 | 2 | | | 7 | 1 | | 3 | | 14 |
| KNP | 1 | 2 | 2 | | 12 | | | 4 | 11 | | 32 |
| KGP | | 3 | 5 | 1 | 11 | 3 | 5 | 15 | 3 | Mec-4 | 50 |
| CHN | 1 | 1 | 4 | | 13 | 1 | 8 | 6 | 19 | 21 | 74 |
| RKE | 1 | | 3 | 1 (IS) | 1 | 2 | | 12 | | LA-12<br>SPA-4 | 36 |

[L-Librarian, DL-Deputy Librarian, AL-Assistant Librarian, SA-System Analyst, IS-Information Scientist, STA-Senior Technical Assistant, TA-Technical Assistant, LA-Library Assistant, SPA-Semi Professional Assistant, Mec - Mechanic]

Library professionals play a unique role in conducting the different library activities; hence their interest and involvement in adapting new technology tools for the betterment of information support to users would fine tune existing services and start new ones. Table 3.10 highlights the details of staff positions in different grades in IIT libraries. During the survey, the Librarian post was vacant in DLH, GHT and KGP and the situation remains the same in case of the last two. The posts of both DL and AL show minor variations in the different Institutes, their strength varying from three to eight. Specialized computer staff (System Analyst/Information Scientist) for systems administration is present only in KGP and RKE. All the Institutes except GHT have around fifteen technical support staff. With a large number of project, contract and trainee staff, CHN possesses the largest number of staff, crossing 70, while MUM and KGP each have more than 50 staff. KNP, DLH, and RKE have more than 30 but less than 40 staff; however, the number of their contractual, temporary and/or trainee positions to compensate for reduced staff strength is not clear. Computerized housekeeping operations have led to reduced staff requirements in acquisition, processing, circulation and journal sections, but not the staff required for essential manual work in these sections, stack maintenance (with a consistently growing but zero weeded out collection), evening and weekend duty shifts.

## 3.11. COMPUTER HARDWARE

*Table 3.11: Computer Hardware*

| ***Code*** | ***Servers*** | | | ***Multimedia*** | ***PCs*** | ***VT 100/*** | ***Other*** |
|---|---|---|---|---|---|---|---|
| | ***Unix*** | ***Linux*** | ***NT*** | ***PCs*** | | ***Dumb Terminals*** | |
| MUM | | 4 | 2 | 25 | 30 | | |
| DLH | | | 4 | | 37 | 25 | |
| GHT | 1 | | | | 11 | | |
| KGP | 3 | 1 | 2 | 7 | 10 | 30 | |
| RKE | | | 2 | 15 | 20 | | CD Servers-2 |

Computers and other IT gadgets are increasingly being used in libraries to conduct computerized information organization and provide IT enabled services. Status of these facilities helps assess the preparedness of libraries to design and implement state of the art information services. Table 3.11 shows the strength of computer hardware in different IIT libraries. All the libraries have a relatively superior infrastructure of servers and computers/ terminals to access the OPAC and various electronic resources available. Since these institutes have state of the art LAN and computer infrastructure in the different departments, many users access the resources through the intranet also. GHT and KGP have Unix servers, MUM and KGP Linux servers, and most have NT/Windows servers. All the Institutes have a good number of old as well as new PCs. However, DLH and KGP also have dumb terminals to access the library OPAC.

## 3.12. COMPUTER SOFTWARE

*Table 3.12: Computer Software*

| *Code* | *Operating System* | *Library Automation* | *Word Processing* | *Database* |
|---|---|---|---|---|
| MUM | DOS, Windows Linux | In-house | Office | mySQL Oracle 8i |
| DLH | | LibSys | | |
| GHT | Windows | LibSys | Office | |
| KNP | | In-house | | |
| KGP | DOS Windows Linux Unix HP Ux | LibSys | Office | DBase, mySQL Oracle 8i |
| RKE | | Troodon | | |

IIT libraries use a wide variety of software for various applications and knowing about these helps to assess the level of IT proficiency among its staff. Table 3.12 details the software used in different IIT Libraries. MUM uses Linux and Microsoft operating systems, GHT uses only windows, while KGP uses a wide variety of Unix and Microsoft systems. DLH, GHT, and KGP use LibSys package for housekeeping operations while MUM and KNP utilize in-house packages to handle the same, and RKE uses Troodon software. Most of the Institutes use MS Office for word processing applications.

## 3.13. CURRENT AWARENESS SERVICE (CAS)

*Table 3.13 A: Current Awareness Service from Print Resources*

| *Code* | *Output Format* | *Profile* | *Users* | *Free/ Paid* | *Outside Users also* | *Frequency* |
|---|---|---|---|---|---|---|
| GHT | AACR II | No (Subject based) | Faculty, Technical, Research Scholars, PG, UG | Free | On Demand | Irregular |
| RKE | | No (General) | Faculty | Free | | |

Both Current Awareness Service (CAS) and Selective Dissemination of Information (SDI) services are highly related to content personalization since all these services attempt to alert and update users about new literature in their fields of interest as and when new materials are added to the existing universe of knowledge. Thus knowing about these services helps to assess the success of user specific, profile based and new literature centric activities in a library. Table 3.13 A highlights the status of CAS from print resources in IIT Libraries. GHT and RKE make use of CAS from print resources, GHT offers the same to all categories of users and RKE offers the service to faculty members only.

Table 3.13 B presents the trend of electronic Current Awareness Service in different IIT Libraries. MUM and KGP provide users latest additions to the collection at regular intervals whereas GHT provides the same in a profile based manner on demand only. KGP offers the service only to internal users while MUM and GHT extend the service to outside users as well.

*Table 3.13 B: Current Awareness Service from Electronic Resources*

| *Code* | *Databases* | *Profile* | *Output Format* | *Users* | *Outside Users also* | *Frequency* |
|---|---|---|---|---|---|---|
| MUM | INSPEC<br>CA on CD<br>ISTP<br>DA<br>Latest additions of books, pamphlets, reports, standards etc. | No | | Faculty, Research Scholars | Yes | Weekly, Fort-nightly |
| GHT | LibSys | Yes | AACR II | Faculty, Technical, Research Scholars, PG, UG | Yes | On demand |
| KGP | Recent additions of books and journals | No | AACR II/free text | All internal users | No | Weekly by email and on Web site |

## 3.14. SELECTIVE DISSEMINATION OF INFORMATION (SDI) SERVICE

*Table 3.14: Electronic SDI Service*

| *Code* | *Databases* | *Users* | *Frequency* | *In-house/ Commercial* | *Output* | *Usage* |
|---|---|---|---|---|---|---|
| MUM | CCOD | Faculty, Research Scholars | Weekly | In-house | Bibliog-raphic | Heavy |

Table 3.14 provides details of electronic SDI service in the IITs. None of the IIT libraries responded to the question regarding the use of printed SDI service. However, senior staff

members in a few libraries remarked that before the advent of electronic databases, preparation of bibliographies and documentation lists was more common. This holds true particularly when faculty members and researchers secure a research project or start research in a new area. MUM provides an electronic SDI service to its faculty and research scholars on a weekly basis and reports heavy usage rate. KGP provided monthly SDI service in 1997 and 1998 using Current Contents on Diskette (CCOD) and operated it using profiles constructed from terms suggested by faculty. However, it was discontinued later due to cancellation of the database subscription and as a result of content alerts from publishers. Electronic journals and table of content alerts by premier journals further enabled researchers to keep abreast of both latest and forthcoming publications in their chosen fields of interest without depending on the library. Such alerting services from publishers might be one reason why other IIT libraries are not venturing into SDI services.

## 3.15. CD-ROM DATABASE SERVICE

*Table 3.15 A: CD-ROM Databases*

| *Code* | *CD-ROM Databases* |
|---|---|
| MUM | INSPEC, OnDisc, ISTP, Dissertation Abstract, CA on CD, ANBAR, Powder Diffraction File (PDF) |
| RKE | Compendex, INSPEC, MathSci, Water Resources Abstracts, Biotechnology Abstracts, Citis, Appl. S&T Abst., Business & Management Practices, Int. Construction Database, Metadex, Georef |
| DLH | Compendex, INSPEC, MathSci, Derwent Biotechnology Abstracts, World Textile, Business Periodical Index, Exim India, LISA Plus, Induscope, IBID, Indian Standards, NUCSSI |
| CHN | Ei Compendex Plus, INSPEC, Current Research Worldwide, Espace World, Findex, and Grants Database. |
| KGP | NUCSSI, IEL, INSPEC, Ei Tech Index, Ei Compendex, Derwent Biotechnology Abstracts, Dialog OnDisc Biotechnology and Bioengineering, Chemical Abstracts, CAB Abstracts, LISA, ITU-T, ITU-R, ASTM standards, BIS, ABI/Inform |

The IITs hold archival data of several electronic databases in CD-ROMs, with a few Institutes providing access to this data over the Intranet. Some of these databases could be also used as content for the personalization service if such data is currently inaccessible through the web. Table 3.15 A summarizes the CD-ROM databases available in the different IIT Libraries. INSPEC is available in five of the IIT Libraries, Compendex in four of the libraries, Biotechnology Abstracts in three of the libraries, and MathSci in two of the libraries. The different Libraries also have certain unique databases relevant to the specialized research and teaching activity undertaken in the individual Institutes.

*Table 3.15 B: CD-ROM Search Services*

| ***Code*** | ***Profile*** | ***Users*** | ***Search by*** | ***Frequency*** | ***Output Sent Through email*** |
|---|---|---|---|---|---|
| MUM | No | Faculty, Technical, Research Scholars, Postgraduate Student (PG), Undergraduate Student (UG) | Library Professionals | Weekly | Yes |
| GHT | No | Faculty, Technical, Research Scholars, PG. UG | Users | On demand | No |
| RKE | No | Faculty, Technical, Research Scholars, PG. UG | Users | On demand | No |
| KGP | No | Faculty, Technical, Research Scholars, PG. UG | Users | On demand | No |

Acquisition of electronic products and introduction of new services reflects the aggressive approach adopted by the library towards various information activities. If a library is proactive in providing such services, it may not find it difficult to get equally involved in techno-centric services like personalization. Table 3.15 B provides details relating to the CD-ROM search services offered by IIT Libraries. The libraries of all the IITs have extended this service to the entire spectrum of internal users including students, faculty, research and technical staff. No library is currently using profiles to operate this service and all except MUM encourage users to conduct the search themselves. MUM even sends weekly outputs of searches conducted by library professionals to users through email.

## 3.16. FULL TEXT INFORMATION SERVICE

*Table 3.16: Full Text Information Services*

| *Code* | *Databases* | *Profile* | *Users* | *Searched by* | *Frequency* | *Output Sent Through email* |
|---|---|---|---|---|---|---|
| MUM | Online E-journals | No | Faculty | Library Professionals | Weekly | Yes |
| KGP | Full Text Databases such as IEL and standards, electronic journals | No | Faculty, Technical, Research Scholars, PG, UG | Users | On demand | No |

Full text resources form the bulk of the content required for personalization services and IIT libraries possessed such resources well before the advent of web access to e-journals. Table 3.16 highlights the status of full text information services offered by different Institutes. MUM provides through email a weekly list of electronic journals to faculty members. KGP has certain standards and full text CD-ROM databases like IEEE/IEE Electronic Library (IEL) in addition to electronic journals. The remaining respondents have apparently not considered the availability of full text databases and electronic journals in their respective libraries and hence not responded to this question.

## 3.17. USER PREFERENCE

*Table 3.17 A: Impact of User Preference on Collection Development and Services*

| *Code* | *Impact of user preference on collection development of books/journals/other sources* | *Impact of user preference on library and information services* |
|---|---|---|
| MUM | Yes | No |
| GHT | Yes, for resource building | |
| KGP | Users decide what new resources are to be purchased | Yes |
| RKE | Gives due weightage to user opinion | |

Users are the best judges of service, and the library being a premier service institution in an academic/research institute is no exception to this rule. The acutely complex nature of research activity in various science and technology fields requires enough domain knowledge to judge the acquisition of information sources. Thus modern libraries involved with higher education/ research always engage users in collection development and access arrangement activities. User feedback and preference are also continuously sought to fine tune existing services and initiate new ones. Table 3.17 A illustrates feedback regarding user preference on collection development and information services. It is evident that the IIT libraries attach considerable importance to user preferences in these activities. All the libraries which responded to this query stated that they routinely considered users' opinions before procuring new books, journals and other types of resources. MUM stated that the services were rendered irrespective of user preference. KGP considered user opinion for providing various services, starting new ones, improving the existing ones and dropping the less popular ones.

*Table 3.17 B: Opinion about User Interest Management*

| ***Code*** | ***Opinion about user interest management*** | ***Interacting through questionnaires/ web forms about library organization and services*** |
|---|---|---|
| MUM | User interest options are always welcome, implemented after the decision of management and staff | Yes |
| GHT | Very positive | No |
| KGP | Highly desirable to justify resources spent for users' information requirements. Presently difficult to handle in an integrated manner due to the diversity of systems and products used to provide different services | Yes |
| RKE | We are all for user interest management | Sometimes |

Libraries should adopt a positive outlook towards managing user interests if they want to satisfy users as per the fundamental laws of library science. A proper estimate and functional representation of user interests is of crucial importance to personalization service. Table 3.17 B describes the various IIT libraries opinions of regarding user interest management and the tools and techniques used to elicit details of users. All the libraries which responded to were unanimously emphatic about the utility of better user interest management along with efficient electronic information systems. It is also evident that the present scenario of products and services from a variety of providers makes it desirable to work with different subsystems for creating and manipulating user interests and profiles. MUM and KGP regularly interact with users through questionnaires/forms about library activities while RKE does it occasionally.

*Table 3.17C: Implicit Use*

| *Code* | *Issue patterns considered in new acquisitions apart from written requisitions* | *Books taken out in reading halls marked for use* | *Photocopy from books and journals estimated for future acquisitions* |
|---|---|---|---|
| MUM | No | No | Books with missing/ torn pages are replaced |
| GHT | No | No | Sometimes |
| RKE | Not at present | No | No |
| KGP | Difficult to practice with the existing staff structure. Number of existing copies are considered while ordering additional copies of textbooks | Around 10 reading halls and no technical staff in stack. Hence not feasible at present | Number of photocopies recorded for administrative purpose. Subject estimate not made due to operational difficulties |

For a functional user interest management system, apart from explicit options, use characteristics are to be estimated through implicit means. Data gathered about implicit use would help the library in fine-tuning user profiles and visibly improving profile based library services. Table 3.17 C lists responses relating to implicit use assessment. An efficient user-interest gathering scheme must also consider implicit use of library resources apart from explicit use characteristics. Some of the methods to gather implicit use of library resources take into account book issue patterns to assess user demands regarding the type of resources, accordingly giving preference to new resources of that type. Apart from user requisitions, books taken out for consultation in reading halls by users are to be quantified to suggest more new resources of that type/subject, and photocopies made from books and journals estimated to improve the quality of new acquisitions. All the libraries which responded to this question stated that they were not considering this in the present context due to operational difficulties and considering existing staff structure and other priorities.

*Table 3.17 D: User Profiles*

| ***Code*** | ***Interacting with users through questionnaires/ Input through web forms, etc., for profile construction and modification*** | ***Are you constructing user profiles to match user preferences? If yes, for what types of services*** | ***Mechanism used to construct user profiles*** |
|---|---|---|---|
| MUM | Yes, web based form is provided | Yes, CCOD Alert | |
| GHT | No | No | |
| KGP | Yes | Yes, for personalizing electronic content | Indirect and direct methods |
| RKE | No | | |

In a higher education and research library, users form a varied group with different subject interests. Hence proper representation of the level and style of resources required by each one of them helps. This is possible only if the users' interests are characterized accordingly. Table 3.17 D presents the preferred modes of collecting user specializations by these libraries for preparing user profiles. MUM and KGP interact with users through questionnaires for profile construction whereas GHT and RKE do not make use of profiles. MUM uses profiles for its CCOD Alert service while KGP is doing the same for personalizing electronic content. KGP constructs profiles both directly by collecting terms of interests from users and indirectly by collecting them from different in-house publications, websites etc., and by automatically constructing the profiles by assessing user interaction with the personalization engine.

*Table 3.17 E: User Profiles 2*

| *Code* | *Steps for optimizing profiles* | *Tools and techniques used for profile construction, modification and tuning* | *Usage from ILL/ Resource Sharing Unit, Reprography Section etc., considered in the construction of user profiles* |
|---|---|---|---|
| MUM | | | Yes |
| KGP | Evaluation of results returned by the system, user feedback etc. | Web based interface for personalization along with proprietary search software | No |

Table 3.17 E highlights the following: steps for optimizing profiles; tools and techniques for profile construction, modification and tuning. It also throws light on whether usage from ILL/Resource Sharing unit, Reprography Section etc., is taken into account during profile construction. MUM uses records maintained at its ILL/Resource Sharing and Reprography Sections for profile construction whereas KGP does not consider it currently feasible, preferring to use instead a web-based interface along with the proprietary software of individual e-resources for construction, modification and tuning of user profiles.

*Table 3.17 F: User Profile 3*

| *Code* | *Mechanisms used to assess and quantify use patterns* | *Opinion for and against incorporating use behavior in profiles* | *Are Artificial Intelligence (AI) techniques used for dynamic modification and optimization?* |
|---|---|---|---|
| MUM | Institute name and address | | |
| KGP | Downloads | Use behavior must be added | Not at present |

Table 3.17 F summarizes the responses received for additional questions about user profiles. MUM identifies use patterns from Institute address and KGP does the same by assessing web downloads. KGP further expressed the view that use behavior must be reflected in profiles. Artificial Intelligence techniques and data mining applications are yet to be started, being presently involved in creating database of holdings and enabling access to acquired, subscribed and licensed resources.

## 3.18. CONTENT PERSONALIZATION AND IIT LIBRARIES

*Table 3.18 A: Content Personalization*

| *Code* | *Awareness* | | *Activities* |
|---|---|---|---|
| | *Yes* | *No* | |
| MUM | Yes | | Profile based search results from CCOD (ECT, PCES, and LS) sent via email to faculty and researchers |
| GHT | Yes | | No |
| KGP | Yes | | Yes, content personalization of electronic full text information for Institute faculty |
| RKE | Yes | | No, currently focusing on user education programmes, web enhancement and digital library of archives |

Tables 3.18 to 3.20 deal with various aspects of content personalization practiced in the IIT libraries. Table 3.18 A reports whether the libraries are aware of content personalization and any specific activities are currently practiced in this regard. MUM, GHT, KGP and RKE are aware of content personalization, but only MUM and KGP have started such services. MUM provides profile based search results from the bibliographic Current Contents database through email while KGP operates the profile based personalized service through web, utilizing full text resources.

*Table 3.18 B: Willingness to Personalize Content*

| *Code* | *1* | *2* | *3* | *4* | *5* | *6* | *7* | *8* |
|---|---|---|---|---|---|---|---|---|
| GHT | ✓ | ✓ | | | ✓ | ✓ | ✓ | Helps develop separate sections for personalized services |
| KGP | ✓ | | ✓ | ✓ | ✓ | | ✓ | Saves the time of researchers during information collection activities |
| RKE | | | | | | | | Not possible in the present manpower scenario |

[1-Large amounts of content procured are unused, 2-A small part of acquired content is not being used properly, 3-Difficult to satisfy user demand otherwise, 4-Difficult to attract users otherwise, 5- Available electronic content can be easily personalized, 6-Leads to Co-operative Collection Management, 7-Improves the image of Library, 8-Other Reasons]

Table 3.18 B highlights responses received against the query regarding willingness to personalize content. RKE expressed its inability to do so in the present inadequate manpower scenario. Though GHT has not initiated any personalization services, it has nevertheless stated certain advantages of such services. KGP provides personalization services citing various reasons like easiness to personalize electronic contents, improve content usage, attract users and satisfy user demands, improve the image of library and enable researchers to save time spent in information collection activity.

Table 3.18 C: Reasons for not Personalizing Content

| *Code* | *1* | *2* | *3* | *4* | *5* | *[1-Importance not felt, 2-Lack of Infrastructure, 3-Inadequate Funds, 4-Lack of Co-operation from Management, 5-Inadequate Staff]* |
|---|---|---|---|---|---|---|
| GHT | | ✓ | | ✓ | ✓ | |
| RKE | | | | | ✓ | |

Table 3.18 C lists the reasons stated by IIT libraries for not personalizing content. GHT is not interested in personalizing content due to lack of infrastructure, low level of cooperation from the management and inadequate staff. RKE too does not have adequate staff to venture into personalization services.

*Table 3.18D: Benefits of Content Personalization*

| Code | 1 | 2 | 3 | 4 | 5 | 6 | 7 | 8 | 9 |
|---|---|---|---|---|---|---|---|---|---|
| MUM | | | | | ✓ | ✓ | ✓ | ✓ | |
| GHT | ✓ | ✓ | ✓ | ✓ | ✓ | ✓ | ✓ | ✓ | Help build special interest groups |
| KGP | ✓ | ✓ | ✓ | ✓ | ✓ | ✓ | | ✓ | Highly relevant collection and more satisfied users |
| RKE | ✓ | ✓ | ✓ | ✓ | ✓ | ✓ | ✓ | ✓ | |

[1-Pin-pointed provision of information to users, 2-Users exposed to highly relevant content, 3-Users need to scan only a portion of the collection, 4- Library collection put to better use, 5-Improved collection development policies, 6-Enhanced use of library content, 7-Cooperative Collection Management, 8-Staff Training, 9-Others]

Table 3.18 D lists the benefits of content personalization as perceived by these libraries. GHT and RKE opted for all the benefits suggested in the questionnaire (pin-pointed provision of information, highly relevant content, users need to scan only a portion of the collection, better use of library collection, improved collection development policies, enhanced use of library content, cooperative collection management, staff training). KGP did not perceive cooperative collection development as a benefit of content personalization while MUM felt the same about the following: pinpointed provision of information, highly relevant content, users need to scan only a portion of the collection, and better use of library collection. GHT maintained that personalization would help build special interest groups, and KGP proposed that the library would acquire a highly relevant collection with more satisfied users as a result of personalization.

*Table 3.18 E: Extending CAS & SDI Techniques to Content Personalization*

| ***Code*** | ***How can CAS and SDI techniques be extended to content personalization?*** | ***Tools and techniques used for content personalization*** |
|---|---|---|
| KGP | Very related as both electronic CAS and SDI use profiles and bibliographic databases in electronic form; personalization also uses profiles, however, the content must be full text databases instead of abstracts/indexes | Full text electronic databases like e-journals, web accessed resources, profile management systems in a web enabled environment for search and retrieval of contents using native search engines of respective resources |
| RKE | Not possible to explain at present | |

Table 3.18 E enumerates feedback regarding the similarity of content personalization with current awareness and selective dissemination services and the specific tools and techniques used for the process. RKE was unable to explain how CAS and SDI techniques could be extended to content personalization. KGP replied that profiles were common to all these services, with variation in only the type of content, since personalization services concentrate on handling full text information.

*Table 3.18 F: Library Section Conducting Personalization*

| ***Code*** | ***Separate Section or Division*** | | ***Section(s) Conducting Personalization Services*** |
|---|---|---|---|
| | ***Yes*** | ***No*** | |
| MUM | | No | Reference and Computers |
| KGP | Yes | | Taken up as part of an MHRD research project |
| RKE | | No | |

Table 3.18 F presents information regarding the section(s) conducting personalization services in IIT libraries. In higher

education institutions like the IITs, libraries are expected to render several traditional services like arranging for books and journals and providing other essential services. Value addition and special services will emerge only in the second stage after providing these basic and essential services. MUM provides personalization through its 'Reference and Computer Application Section' whereas it has been taken up as part of an MHRD project in KGP.

*Table 3.18 G: Hardware for Personalization*

| ***Code*** | ***Linux Servers*** | ***NT Servers*** | ***NT Works-tations*** | ***Multi-media PCs*** | ***PCs*** | ***VT 100 Terminals*** | ***Any other*** |
|---|---|---|---|---|---|---|---|
| MUM | | | | | ✓ | | |
| KGP | 1 | | | 1 | | | |

Table 3.18 G lists the hardware used for personalization work in the IIT libraries. MUM uses PCs as hardware for personalization while KGP has Linux server and client access through PCs connected to the intranet.

*Table 3.18 H: Software for Personalization*

| ***Code*** | ***Operating System*** | ***Automation Software*** | ***Database Software*** | ***Networking Software*** |
|---|---|---|---|---|
| MUM | DOS<br>Windows | In-house | CCOD | Linux |
| KGP | Linux<br>Windows | Apache Web server. PHP programs | Electronic journals, INDEST resources | |

Table 3.18 H presents details regarding the software used for content personalization. MUM uses DOS and Windows operating system, in-house automation software and CCOD bibliographic database. KGP makes use of Linux and windows operating systems, apache web server, PHP programming and content such as electronic journals and INDEST resources.

*Table 3.18 I: Content for Personalization*

| **Code** | **Printed** | **Electronic** | | | | |
|---|---|---|---|---|---|---|
| | | ***Book Floppies/ CDs*** | ***Bibliographic Databases*** | ***Full Text Databases*** | ***Electronic Journals*** | ***Internet/ Web Resources*** |
| MUM | | | ✓ | | | |
| KGP | | | | ✓ | ✓ | ✓ |

Table 3.18 I lists the sources of content used for providing personalization service. It can be seen that while MUM utilizes bibliographic databases, KGP uses full text databases, electronic journals and Internet/web resources.

*Table 3.18 J: Delivery Mode of Personalized Content*

| **Code** | **Printed** | **Electronic** | | |
|---|---|---|---|---|
| | | ***Over LAN*** | ***Through Email*** | ***Through Website*** |
| MUM | | | ✓ | |
| KGP | | | | ✓ |

Table 3.18 J throws light on the mode used by IIT Libraries to deliver personalized content to their users. MUM supplies the results through email whereas KGP hosts the matched results in researchers' personalized web pages stored in the personalization server.

*Table 3.18 K: Staff for Personalization*

| ***Code*** | ***Assistant Librarian*** | ***Others*** |
|---|---|---|
| MUM | 1 | |
| KGP | 1 | Project Assistant |

Table 3.18 K supplies details regarding the staff responsible for conducting the personalization service. KGP utilizes one Assistant Librarian and a Project Assistant to provide the service while MUM operates the service with the help of one Assistant Librarian.

*Table 3.18 L: Budget for Content Personalization*

| Code | Percentage of budget spent | Budget spent on content personalization products and services is More than appropriate | Appropriate | Less than appropriate |
|---|---|---|---|---|
| MUM | | | ✓ | |
| KGP | 1 | | ✓ | |

Table 3.18 L records the respondents' opinions regarding the budget spent for content personalization. KGP spends about less than 1% of the total library budget for personalization. Both MUM and KGP opined that the budget spent for personalization service was appropriate.

*Table 3.18 M: Source Data for Content Personalization*

| Code | 1 | 2 | 3 | 4 | 5 | 6 |
|---|---|---|---|---|---|---|
| MUM | ✓ | | | | | |
| KGP | ✓ | | | | | Information about faculty specialization in the annual and research reports and Institute website, key words from faculty publications etc. |

[1-Online/offline forms, Library usage history: 2- Based on books issued, 3-Based on books requested, 4- Based on articles photocopied, 5- Based on articles referred, 6- Any other]

Table 3.18 M presents sources of data for constructing profile used in content personalization. MUM and KGP collected source data (especially for profile construction and identification of potential content) from online/offline forms. KGP used certain internal sources as well to refine these specializations including annual and research reports, Institute website, key words from publications etc.

*Table 3.18 N: Components of Content Personalization*

| ***Code*** | ***Content management*** | ***Data Mining*** | ***Use Characteristics*** | ***Data Intelligence*** |
|---|---|---|---|---|
| MUM | ✓ | ✓ | | |
| KGP | ✓ | ✓ | ✓ | ✓ |

Table 3.18 N presents the components of content personalization. MUM suggested content management and data mining while KGP regarded use characteristics and data intelligence too as essential.

## 3.19. IMPACT OF CONTENT PERSONALIZATION

*Table 3.19 A: Impact of Content Personalization on Library Professionals*

| ***Code*** | ***Day-to-day Work*** | | | ***Efficiency*** | | | ***Productivity*** | | |
|---|---|---|---|---|---|---|---|---|---|
| | ***Posi-tive*** | ***Nega-tive*** | ***Nil*** | ***Posi-tive*** | ***Nega-tive*** | ***Nil*** | ***Posi-tive*** | ***Nega-tive*** | ***Nil*** |
| MUM | | | | | | | ✓ | | |
| GHT | ✓ | | | ✓ | | | ✓ | | |
| KGP | ✓ | | | ✓ | | | ✓ | | |

Table 3.19 A illustrates the impact of content personalization on library professionals. MUM felt that personalization played a positive role on productivity while GHT and KGP expressed the opinion that it also had a positive impact on day to day work and efficiency. RKE stated that since they did not yet operate any personalization service, it was a hypothetical question and hence could only be answered after observing the real impact.

*Table 3.19 B: Impact of Content Personalization on Library Users*

| ***Code*** | ***Meeting Information Needs*** | | | ***Relation with Library*** | | |
|---|---|---|---|---|---|---|
| | ***Positive*** | ***Negative*** | ***Nil*** | ***Positive*** | ***Negative*** | ***Nil*** |
| MUM | | | | ✓ | | |
| GHT | ✓ | | | ✓ | | |
| KGP | ✓ | | | ✓ | | |

Table 3.19 B enumerates the impact of content personalization on library users. MUM stated that personalization had a positive impact on users' relation with the library. GHT and KGP mentioned that in addition, it exercised a beneficial impact on fulfilling users' information needs.

*Table 3.19 C: Impact of Content Personalization on Information Organization*

| *Code* | *Collection Development* | | | *Information Processing* | | |
|---|---|---|---|---|---|---|
| | *Positive* | *Negative* | *Nil* | *Positive* | *Negative* | *Nil* |
| MUM | ✓ | | | | | |
| GHT | ✓ | | | ✓ | | |
| KGP | ✓ | | | ✓ | | |

Table 3.19 C illustrates the impact of content personalization on information organization. MUM, GHT and KGP expressed the view that personalization exercised a positive impact on collection development. GHT and KGP opined that it has a positive impact on information processing too.

*Table 3.19 D: Impact of Content Personalization on Information Services*

| *Code* | *Quality* | | | *Quantity* | | |
|---|---|---|---|---|---|---|
| | *Positive* | *Negative* | *Nil* | *Positive* | *Negative* | *Nil* |
| MUM | ✓ | | | | | |
| GHT | ✓ | | | | ✓ | |
| KGP | ✓ | | | | ✓ | |

Table 3.19 D summarizes the impact of content personalization on information services. MUM, GHT and KGP confirmed personalization's positive impact on the quality of services provided. Profile-based retrieval may lead to a greater number of articles being retrieved, some of which might not be of much relevance, hence GHT and KGP pointed out the possible negative impact on the quantity of information services.

*Table 3.19 E: Impact of Content Personalization on the Library*

| *Code Impact* | *Library usage* | | | *Image* | | | *Technology Adoption* | | | *Socio-cultural* | | |
|---|---|---|---|---|---|---|---|---|---|---|---|---|
| | *Positive* | *Negative* | *Nil* | *+ve* | *-ve* | *Nil* | *+ve* | *-ve* | *Nil* | *+ve* | *-ve* | *Nil* |
| MUM | ✓ | | | | | | | | | | | |
| GHT | ✓ | | | ✓ | | | ✓ | | | ✓ | | |
| KGP | ✓ | | | ✓ | | | ✓ | | | | | |

Table 3.19 E evaluates the impact of content personalization on the library as a whole. MUM, GHT, and KGP were of the opinion that content personalization exercises a positive impact on library usage, while GHT and KGP stated that it affects in a positive manner both the library's image and new technology adoption. GHT commented on its beneficial impact on sociocultural relations as well.

### 3.19.1. Effects of Content Personalization

*Table 3.19 F: Effects of Content Personalization*

| *Code* | *Library Services* | | | *User satisfaction* | | | *Meeting Users' Demands* | | | *Library Materials Usage* | | | *Library Image* | | |
|---|---|---|---|---|---|---|---|---|---|---|---|---|---|---|---|
| | > | < | = | > | < | = | > | < | = | > | < | = | > | < | = |
| MUM | ✓ | | | ✓ | | | | | | ✓ | | | ✓ | | |
| GHT | ✓ | | | ✓ | | | ✓ | | | ✓ | | | ✓ | | |
| KGP | ✓ | | | ✓ | | | ✓ | | | ✓ | | | ✓ | | |

[> Improve, <Don't Improve, = Remain the same]

Table 3.19 F throws light on the impact of content personalization on various areas. MUM, GHT and KGP were of the opinion that library services, user satisfaction, material usage and library image would significantly improve after implementing personalization services. GHT and KGP also supported its effect in meeting the various user demands.

## 3.19.2. Future Plans

*Table 3.19 G: Future Plans*

| Code | Future Plans | Additional Information |
|---|---|---|
| GHT | Depend on the natural growth of the Library | Similar institutions of north east imparting courses should be regularly targeted and networked as their users need definite collection and information availability |
| KGP | Transferring personalization service from a project mode to regular library service, Extending the service to all categories of users, Building a digital library of internal contents, Setting up an institutional repository of institute publications etc. | With INDEST resources accessible in all IITs, KGP's personalization service can be replicated in other IITs, or individual IITs can post their user profiles on the KGP SAI personalization server to extend the services to users in other IITs |
| RKE | Nothing at present | |

Table 3.19 G highlights future plans of the IIT Libraries concerning content personalization. GHT proposes to adopt personalization as a future activity depending on the natural growth of the library, calling for enhanced networking and collaboration with other institutions in the north east. KGP aims to transfer personalization service from a project mode to regular library service to fulfill three objectives. These include extending the service to all categories of users, creating a digital library of internal contents and setting up an institutional repository of institute publications etc. KGP also feels that there is a strong case for extending its personalization service to the other IITs. This can be accomplished either by replicating the service at different Institutes or by posting user profiles from the other IITs into the KGP Specialized Access to Information (SAI) personalization server. This is particularly feasible in the current scenario since a major chunk of electronic resources are now commonly accessible following the setting up of the INDEST consortium

### 3.19.3. Problems and Solutions

*Table 3.19 H: Problems and Solutions*

| *Code* | *Problems* | *Suggestions and Solutions* |
|---|---|---|
| GHT | Shortage of staff<br>Lack of infrastructure | Each library should have individual infrastructure for rendering modern services in a competitive environment |
| KGP | Diverse interfaces of different electronic products prohibiting a single window search and selective retrieval | Licensing agreements must explore the provision of copying and local serving of contents through a local search engine |
| | Academically busy researchers unable to spare much time for fine tuning profiles, hampering both retrieval precision and optimum use | Client side personalization and indirect techniques must be augmented to fine tune the profiles since there is a remote chance of users spending more time interacting with the system during their highly competitive and acutely busy schedules. |

Table 3.19 H highlights the major problems and possible solutions identified by the IIT libraries in operating personalization services. GHT mentioned shortage of staff and lack of infrastructure as the major obstacles faced in personalizing contents. KGP listed factors like different electronic product interfaces (e.g. Elsevier ScienceDirect, IEEE/IEE Electronic Library, ACM Digital Library etc.) prohibiting cross search, and inadequate user feedback, as primary reasons for hindering personalization. It further proposed local serving of different databases through in-house search engines to overcome proprietary search engines, and evolving proxy based techniques for indirect observation of user interaction to construct and refine profiles as viable solutions.

The analysis reveals that all the libraries are equipped with relatively superior collection, infrastructure and services. This confirms the validity as well as desirability of taking the library of one Institute as a model to explore the feasibility of implementing personalization services in all the Institutes. Knowledge regarding users and their appropriate representation into the system being extremely important for proper framing of personalization services, which is discussed in detail in the following chapter.

## REFERENCES

1. **Arora,** Jagdish and **Agrawal**, Pawan, Indian Digital Library in Engineering Science and Technology (INDEST) Consortium: Consortia-Based Subscription to Electronic Resources for Technical Education System in India: A Government of India Initiative, International CALIBER 2003, Ahmedabad, 13-15 February 2003, Conference Volume - Mapping Technology on Libraries and People, Ahmedabad: INFLIBNET, 2003, pp. 271-290.

# Chapter 4
# User Interest Management System

## 4.0. INTRODUCTION

Besides content, a library personalization system needs a highly effective and actively functional user interest handling system to take care of researchers' complex inter and intra disciplinary specializations. A library is different from a publisher's warehouse or a bookshop due to the immense intellectual effort involved in the collection development exercise. It aims to ideally showcase a diverse, lively, dynamic and 'something for everyone' selection from the mass of information produced. Nowadays, due to the much talked about information explosion and budget crunch, no library is able to procure the entire amount of relevant information published in the subject areas of interest to an institution. In this scenario, libraries have evolved various criteria to ensure a functional collection by involving users as active participants in collection development, striving to make increased use of what is being procured with the limited funds available. Usage quantification is thus the best way to evaluate the utility of information resources procured in a library. With printed sources, it has been always difficult to assess the actual use, as most of the manual records and usage statistics from library automation systems fail to provide micro level usage reports. Perhaps libraries have to redesign their user interaction measurement and use quantification tools and techniques to obtain a realistic estimate about what is being used out of what is procured/accessed. A probable reason for lack of sufficient use of library is either the irrelevance or incompleteness of collection to user need or the absence of suitable alerting services to regularly inform and update users about what is being procured. Content personalization systems have a major role to play in this regard.

Library science works on the principle of classifying and arranging information resources of interest to users and devising effective and efficient techniques for their selective retrieval. Thus, profiling users or managing user interests is as important as collection development and access management activities. In a library, along with collection and staff, users form the vital link in the information consumption chain, the former two ideally existing only for the latter. The personalization tasks would be able to deliver qualitative and quantitative usage parameters, indirectly acting as vital evaluation tools for the utility of library resources. Further, for an improved personalization system, an effective user mapping system is second only to useful contents, leading to enhanced use of electronic resources.

Not many serious studies have so far been conducted on the actual use of sources procured in libraries which utilize national resources and a significant amount of professional time. Managing user interests in the context of the progress libraries have made in the processing and management of printed and electronic resources is not an easy task. This is primarily due to the difficulties inherent in handling intelligent and thinking human beings with diverse backgrounds and multiple interests. The Second and Third Laws of Library Science emphasize both enhanced use of the sources acquired and providing users the right source demanded by them. In the absence of intensive personal information support, users (especially researchers working under extreme pressure to deliver solutions relating to various mission oriented consultancy and research projects) will be left to fend for themselves. They will then be forced to scan the information overload through library OPACs (Online Public Access Catalogues), commercial electronic databases and other sources. This may often lead to information under-use, significantly impacting the research and development output and its quality, with the right sources not reaching the right person at the right time.

## 4.1. INFORMATION NEEDS

Science is broadly defined as "knowledge acquired by study, acquaintance with or mastery of any department of learning" or "a branch of study which is concerned either with a connected body of demonstrated truths or with observed facts systematically classified... and which includes trustworthy methods for the discovery of new truth...". Engineering is the work done by or the profession of an engineer who is "designing and constructing works of public utility", whereas technology is defined as "the scientific study of practical or industrial arts" (all quotes from The Oxford English Dictionary, 2nd ed., Oxford: Clarendon, 1989). The study of science lays greater emphasis on studying and characterizing scientific facts, whereas synthesizing new products and techniques is the major thrust in engineering and technology. Hence it is argued that scientists create new knowledge whereas engineers and technologists focus on new things, new chemicals or new machines (**Price**, 1989). These differing perceptions can be aptly summarized in the following words: "scientists and technologists work in fiercely competitive worlds, but in science competition is among individuals for prestige, and in technology, it is among corporations for profit" (**Ladendorf**, 1970). Scientists' work may be grouped under the different stages of *observation* (collecting relevant information), *hypothesis* (formulating a tentative theory to interpret the observed facts), *experimental* (designing and carrying out controlled tests to confirm the hypothesis) and *conclusion* (formulating an answer to the problem when experiments prove the theory) (**Grogan**, 1976). Over the years, the distinction between pure science and its applied variants of engineering and technology has been slowly fading; both disciplines progressively exhibiting similar traits in study, research and teaching. A lot of pure science researchers are now doing technological (applied) research; the widespread mission oriented research practiced in contrast to the erstwhile pure and discipline oriented research contributing primarily to this symbiosis. In contrast to other disciplines, Science and Technology (S&T) being a cherished area of practice, its progress depends to a large extent on the awareness and utilization of existing knowledge; hence the tasks of identifying, selecting and digesting pertinent information from the flood of existing literature are extremely crucial (**Subramanyam**, 1979).

Information need is what an individual *ought* to have; want is what an individual *would* like to have; demand is what an individual *asks* for; use is what an individual actually *uses*; and requirement denotes *what is needed, what is wanted or what is demanded* (**Line**, 1974). Information needs are affected by a variety of factors like the range of sources available, the uses to which information will be put, the user's individual characteristics, social, political and economic systems surrounding the user, and the consequences of information use (**Paisley**, 1968). Information required for research can be classified into *conceptual* (relating to concepts and ideas), *empirical* (either reported by someone or observed by the researcher), *procedural* (methods that are part of a given set of problems) and *stimulatory* (activities moving in the direction of work on a particular problem) (**Hertz** and **Rubenstein**, 1978). As far as information needs are concerned, *visceral need* is the vague sense of a gap in knowledge expressed only by vague dissatisfaction. When an ill-defined area of indecision is given a conscious mental description, it becomes the *conscious need*. When the need is more precise and expressed as a formalized statement, it is treated as the *formalized need* whereas when the user compromises the need in terms of the capabilities of the source, it is termed as the *compromised need* (**Taylor**, 1968). The three dominant approaches to information adopted by a scientist may be termed as *current*, *everyday* and *exhaustive* (**Voight**, 1961). The need to keep up to date with current progress in a field or the need to know what others have recently done or are doing in a specific field or broader area is considered the *current* approach. Many a time, the need for a bit of data, a method, an equation, an explanation of a phenomena or many similar aids is felt by the scientist during the course of research; this is called the *everyday* approach. Before starting a new investigation, publishing results or filing patents, it becomes increasingly important to check through the entire existing information relevant to a given subject as exhaustively as possible. This process of information collection is termed the *exhaustive* approach (**Voight**, 1961). To these three approaches can be added the *browsing* approach to represent the discovery of useful items not looking for, using chance as an informal kind of random sampling (**Grogan**, 1976).

Scientists spend 50-60% of their time communicating (**Björk** and **Turk**, 2000). Scholarly articles are identified for reading in five basic ways: *browsing, automated searches, citations found in the literature, mention by other people and current-awareness tools* (**Tenopir** and **King**, 1998). By and large, the requirement in science and technology is normally for unknown sources (sources whose subject only is known as opposed to the author and/or title approach for known documents in humanities). Science and technology disciplines are largely approached by users through subject and the number of publications to be tracked being much more than in other disciplines, the utility of profiles (representing user specializations) to collect relevant information is widely established. Instead of deliberately collecting user specialization for profiling as was common earlier, there are electronic (hidden) methods to assess user interests. Personalization involves gathering user-related information during interaction with the user, which is then used to deliver appropriate content and services, tailor-made to the user's needs (**Hertz** and **Rubenstein**, 1978). Current research on personalization attempts to build a model of the user's interests and preferences over time (**Croft** *et al.*, 1976).

## 4.2. USERS AND THE LIBRARY

Although the proportion of scientists who still browse to identify scholarly articles for reading purpose remains unchanged, an increasing number are using online searches as evidenced by the increasing proportion of readings identified through online searches (**Tenopir** and **King**, 1998). Escalating prices and rising budgetary constraints in recent years have forced library acquisitions to suffer a serious setback, compelling users to look beyond the library for their varied information requirements. Librarians are not yet acting as true consumers and until we do that, we cannot blame predatory publishers for taking advantage of the situation (**Reenen**, 1998). Another issue involves the enormous and ever increasing number of articles obtained through photocopying, interlibrary loan, document delivery, preprints and reprints (**Tenopir** and **King**, 1998). The first step in assessing whether user interest in libraries is depleting is to study use patterns over the years, the key issue being whether libraries and librarians are serious enough to conduct an objective assessment. In a country like India, where the population growth has not yet stabilized and one which is further characterized by poor literacy and weak higher education indices, going by numbers alone will not suffice for any of the qualitative aspects. Although there is no reduction in the number of books issued in an academic library, determining whether the new acquisitions are being used to the same or greater extent requires in-depth analysis. The fall in library attendance is a truer statement of facts in the absence of supporting statistics. Few users actually visit the library, fewer still spend some time in it, and many others prefer to utilize it through photocopies, network accesses etc. Perhaps as professionals we are afraid to look at these issues, as the results of such assessments may force the authorities to critically examine and even cut the investments on a service institution like the library. Like Reenen's observations about librarians being false consumers, it seems that many librarians are afraid of a realistic self-assessment about library use, user evaluation of libraries and performance audits. Going by citations in articles, libraries have to accept the fact that users are seriously getting addicted to web resources. The Proceedings volume of CALIBER (the annual conference of INFLIBNET Centre) 2001 contains 39 papers with 346 references, out of which 157 pertain to electronic information on websites.

## 4.3. NEED AND PURPOSE OF COLLECTING USER INTERESTS

Survey studies reveal what users normally expect in a digital environment (**Jayawardana** *et al.*, 2001):

* Special facilities for customizing, reusing or linking relevant segments in a reference book when using multimedia sources
* Maintenance of the information collected in a personal space (personal library).
* Organization of the information collected according to learning requirements.
* Enhancement of passive reading, watching and listening by annotating, segmenting, modifying and integrating library sources as part of users' knowledge construction.

It is difficult to ascertain what users need and hence a library's information services are primarily based on this subjective input. Users are therefore quite justified in commenting about misses or noise in SDI/CAS/electronic services output. A computerized environment, while undoubtedly increasing the quantum of information available within one's reach, has in no way enhanced users' information consumption skills. Though widely exposed to more microfilms, Xerox copies and electronic information on desktop/Intranet/Web, ready to be displayed at the touch of a button, the more time users spend searching and collecting information, the less time they get to use it. Further, the amount of information one requires to work on a particular problem is subjective, since human beings are known to observe the 'principle of least effort'. Accessibility of information resources is usually assumed to depend on a range of cognitive, social and physical factors, like whether a person is aware of a resource, possess the knowledge and skills needed to access it and has the resource close at hand (**Bishop**, 1998). Perhaps one may easily tide over an information crisis by identifying only 20% of the total references and even by using only 20% of what is identified. Our own experience in professional research suggests that in many cases it is impossible to collect all the information sources available on a particular topic and there is a possibility of bypassing many of them in research and academic endeavors.

## 4.4. FACETS OF USER INTERESTS

Users have attributes, interests, desires and needs – some or all of which need to be captured and processed. Techniques used to complete the picture of the user are varied and may directly or indirectly engage him/her to different degrees (**Bonett**). Although "true" personalization would use a long-term profile or user model to choose contexts, and therefore additional query terms, for each individual user, we believe that context representation and its inference is a basic component of any approach to content personalization (**Croft** *et al.*, 1976). As far as user interest management is concerned, it has not been taken up in an integrated fashion so far. The user database in the library automation system is used only for keeping an inventory of books issued, returned, renewed, or reserved by users. Some libraries might have added a few keywords in the user database to run CAS/SDI of books added to their collections. The CAS/SDI services essentially operate with the help of electronic bibliographic databases as well as detailed user/ user groups' profiles stored in the proprietary database search software. Recommendations from individual users are seriously sought and considered for procuring books and such recommendations on a departmental/groups of department basis definitely influence addition or deletion of journals. But as in other cases, most of these recommendations and user preferences now reside only in the concerned automation software modules and hence do not provide a concrete picture of user interests. Libraries need an integrated user interest management system to carefully account for each and every service. Another issue of concern relates to how continuously user interests are modified in the CAS/SDI profiles to reflect the continuous change in users' subject areas. Apart from expressed needs, many do not consider important in constructing user profiles, most probably due to difficulty in implementation, usage statistics and use behavior from library databases, or records stored at ILL/Resource Sharing unit, Reprography Section etc. In this scenario, one feasible way to identify use is through citations in their articles. However, though a dominant method, citation tracking for use assessment has not yet been utilized by many libraries. There are also certain limitations with citations, since many of them are self-citations or citations from citations in what is read, leading to citing what is not at all used. The major problem areas for citations in the digital realm are both philosophical and physical. The philosophical problem lies in defining the unit carrying scientific contributions: what should be cited, what should be pointed out, while the physical problems concern longevity and authenticity (**Lindquist**, 1999).

## 4.5. TOOLS AND TECHNIQUES FOR COLLECTING USER INTERESTS

Bonett has identified some of the technologies to determine and deliver 'appropriate content' to match user needs. These include:

a) **Fill-in Profile:** Built with active user involvement, typically through fill-in forms.

b) **Click-stream Analysis/ Web Usage Mining Systems:** Used to keep track of visited links.

c) **Collaborative Filtering:** For comparing a user's tastes with those of other users to build up a picture of like-minded people. This technique may be of less significance when categories of users and preferences are already well defined.

d) **Cookies:** The cookie, a small data packet sent by a website and stored on the browser, forms the link to profile-specific information stored on the server side.

Any one of these techniques or a combination of them can be used to extract user preferences as per the individual library's requirements. If personalization's goal is to improve the effectiveness of information access by adapting to individual users' needs, techniques like relevance feedback and filtering could certainly be considered to support personalization (**Croft** *et al.*, 1976). Three dominant modes of eliciting user interests are:

* input through printed forms,
* submission of electronic forms through email, and
* filling up of forms displayed on the website.

And the curious fact is that while some of the interests are expressed, several others have to be assessed and captured through one or more of the following options:

**Online/Offline Forms:** Earlier, printed forms to collect users' subject specializations were circulated before venturing into user specific information services. Nowadays, the same information can be collected through web forms, and the process be made interactive by enabling users to modify terms based on the results retrieved.

**Library Usage History:** Usage by individual users can be explored to refine their subject profiles, for example, what kind of books or journals they are referring to as well as citing, which information they are placing for resource sharing/database search requests etc.

**Artificial Intelligence (AI):** AI techniques may be employed to auto-learn and intelligently refine the subject specializations of individual clients.

## 4.6. USER INTEREST MANAGEMENT SYSTEM IN A LIBRARY

Though many libraries have implemented automation systems and electronic access to full text databases, an integrated user interest management is still not implemented by most of them. Creation of such a system will thus undoubtedly lead to improved and more effective library services.

### 4.6.1. User Interests in Library Automation System

Library housekeeping operations are generally conducted through a proprietary commercial package, which may be restrictive and does not permit interfacing with any other systems or services inside or outside the library. The system may contain contact information about different categories of users and details of books reserved, issued, renewed or returned by them. There may be provisions to enter keywords, author names etc. to run SDI alerts for newly added books. This feature, however, could not effectively be used due to the limited number of books added in a specific subject area in a week or month, and can be substituted by a general alerting feature concerning new arrivals. Although books purchased can be handled through the package, information concerning those who recommend the same may not be properly updated either due to software problems or operational constraints.

### 4.6.2. Scattered User Interests

The Acquisition Section holds the relevant details of users who recommend different books by filling up the requisition forms. Similarly, the Technical Processing Section contains details of new books issued to faculty members on temporary loan basis. In many cases, it is not only the user who recommended books but also others avail this facility. Apart from books issued, there are many other books consulted in the reading areas in the library which are not considered to assess 'who is reading what' due to the difficulties involved in tracking such use. Though books transferred to bindery are recorded in the automation package, relevant qualitative information regarding their maximum usage is not properly assessed. The Non-Book Section handles theses, patents, standards, microforms etc. These items are not normally issued out and the statistics maintained in the Section only reveal facts about who visited the section and who used what for how long. In the case of multipart items, this inventory fails to accurately disclose actual user interests. It may be difficult for the Reference Section to maintain any such records. The ILL/DDS Unit provides items on loan or as photocopies. These pertain to information sources not available in the Library or for purchase in the market or unavailable due to budget constraints, but recommended by users. Though statistics regarding service usage are usually maintained, these are recorded manually on registers and forms in a standalone mode. The official Xerox facility may maintain details of items xeroxed and users who requested them whereas heavily used Xerox facilities maintained by private operators do not maintain any such record other than the number of pages Xeroxed. In the changing perspective of time constrained information at one's fingertips qualitative aspects relating to Xerox facility usage will undoubtedly bring to light usage of information resources, especially costly ones (like journals essential for research) which are not normally issued out like books. The electronic access section may contain information about the service availed by different users in the form of accessing video courses, standalone databases and electronic supplements of printed books in CD-ROMs and floppies.

### 4.6.3. User Interests from Electronic Access

Electronic information is easier to track than information in printed form, despite concerns regarding privacy in the electronic environment. However, there are certain difficulties in obtaining the qualitative use characteristics of information by individual users, mainly due to technical and operational constraints. Since requests for electronic access of journals through subscription/consortia access passes via proxy servers, all requests made from the campus will reflect this Internet Protocol (IP) Address. Normally, publishers provide usage reports based on this proxy IP. Senior level administrators may be satisfied with the Institute's overall usage of resources; however, for implementing a personalized information utility, use by individual researchers needs to be tracked. Since Campus computer resources' security being at stake while bypassing the proxy, another option could be utilized to place the personalization server at a sublevel to campus proxy as an alternative. We could thus track down usage of individual articles from different e-resource portals by individual users whose requests have been forwarded through the personalization server (more details are provided in the implementation part in Chapter 6).

### 4.6.4. User Interests for Library Personalization

It is evident that the objectives of personalization are an extension to full text information utilizing the virtues of web and database technology of what has already been achieved in CAS/SDI with bibliographic information. Hence, to start with the profiles created for previous electronic services like SDI by refining them in the following manner:

a) scanning departmental websites and personal homepages of faculty members to include more subject areas of interest and refine the existing terms

b) building automatic feedback into the system by implementing proxy features in the personalization server

The next chapter discusses the need for standardized terms for representing the subject interests in the profiles to search and retrieve the most relevant results from the different electronic systems. Retrieving the most relevant results has become more crucial in the context of aggressive research practiced by busy researchers in these institutions. Saving their valuable time by providing the most relevant results so that they can be scanned and easily incorporated into the present research is one of the chief merits of personalization systems.

## REFERENCES


1. **Bishop** (Ann Peterson). Logins and Bailouts: Measuring Access, Use, and Success in Digital Libraries. *The Journal of Electronic Publishing*. 4, 2; December 1998. http://www.press.umich.edu/jep/ 04-02/bishop.html

2. **Björk** (Bo-Christer) and **Turk** (Ziga). How Scientists Retrieve Publications: An Empirical Study of How the Internet is Overtaking Paper Media. *The Journal of Electronic Publishing*. 6, 2; December 2000. http://www.press.umich.edu/jep/06-02/bjork.html

3. **Bonett** (Monica). Personalization of Web Services: Opportunities and Challenges. *Ariadne*. 28. http://www.ariadne.ac.uk /issue28/personalization/intro.html

4. **Croft** (W. Bruce) *et al*. Relevance Feedback and Personalization: A Language Modeling Perspective. http://www.ercim.org/publication/ws-proceedings/DelNoe02/croft-delos.pdf

5. **Grogan** (Denis). Science and Technology: An introduction to literature. 3rd rev. ed. 1976. Clive Bingley. London.

6. **Hertz** (D B) and **Rubenstein** (A H). Team Research. 1954. Columbia University, Dept. of Industrial Engineering. New York. (cited in **Lancaster** (F W). Towards Paperless Information Systems. 1978. Academic Press. New York.).

7. **Jayawardana** (Champa K) *et al*. Personalization tools for active learning in Digital Libraries. *MC Journal: The Journal of Academic Media Librarianship*. 8, 1; Summer 2001. wings.buffalo.edu/publications/ mcjrnl/v8n1/active.pdf

8. **Ladendorf** (Janice M). Information Flow in Science, Technology, and Commerce. *Special Libraries*. 61; 1970; 215-222.

9. **Lindquist** (Mats G). Not Your Father's References: Citations in the Digital Space. *The Journal of Electronic*

*Publishing*. 4, 3; March 1999. http://www.press.umich.edu/jep/04-03/lindquist.html

10. **Line** (Maurice B). Draft Definitions: Information and Library needs, wants, demands, and uses. *Aslib Proceedings*. 26, 2; Feb 1974.

11. **Paisley** (W J). Information needs and users. *ARIST*. 3; 1968; 1-30.

12. **Price** (Derek J. De Solla). Measuring the Size of Science. *Proc. Israel Acad. Sciences and Humanities*. 4, 6; 1989; 98-111.

13. **Reenen** (Johann Van). Library Consumerism in the Digital Age. *The Journal of Electronic Publishing*. 3, 3; March 1998. http://www.press.umich.edu/jep/03-03/vanreenen.html

14. **Subramanyam** (K). Scientific Literature. In Encyclopedia of Library and Information Science. 1979. V. 26. Marcel Dekker. New York. p. 382, 391, 392, 394, 396, 400, 433.

15. **Taylor** (R S). Question negotiation and information seeking in libraries. *College and Research Libraries*. 28; 1968; 178-194.

16. **Tenopir** (Carol) and **King** (Donald W). Designing Electronic Journals With 30 Years of Lessons from Print. *The Journal of Electronic Publishing*. 4, 2; December 1998. http:// www.press.umich.edu/jep/04-02/king.html

17. **Voight** (Melvin J). Scientist's Approaches to Information. ACRL Monograph 24. American Library Association. 1961, p 20-33.

# Chapter 5
# Standardizing Subject Terms

## 5.0. INTRODUCTION

The preceding chapter identifies the need and purpose of user interest management to evolve a fully functional content personalization system in a library. Profiles attempt to map researchers' information requirements in the standard vocabulary of the subjects concerned, facilitating the best possible retrievals from the system while eliminating noise to the bare minimum. Thus, a profile meant for Physics researchers would hardly retrieve any resource from an Economics database due to the wide disparities in structuring and usage of terms in these two disciplines. In a personalization system, the objective is to identify current and useful literature at the earliest to aid and supplement the information requirements of practicing academicians and/or researchers. Here the focus is more on precision than recall. The present chapter deals with the different steps arrived at to achieve standardized subject terms to work with the personalization system.

## 5.1. NEED FOR STANDARDIZING SUBJECT TERMS

Any computer-based retrieval system requires carefully selected and workable search terms to selectively separate useful and relevant information from the large amount of information available in a specific branch of knowledge. Most electronic systems use currently in vogue technical terms in the concerned field, and it is always helpful if one sticks to these terms while conducting the search. Also, focusing on standard terms helps avoid the noise and irrelevant retrievals one normally encounters in electronic retrieval systems. The personalization system under development aims to gather the initial input regarding faculty members' and researchers' subject specializations from their websites or home pages highlighting their areas of research, publications, research projects etc. However, the subject specializations mentioned need to be polished and in some cases, laced with context and qualifiers to be linked with other similar or broader terms for improving their utility. Since thesauri and subject heading lists happen to be very exhaustive and hence not essential in the context of a research area description, this study explored authentic alternative standard sources to create standard subject terms for use with the personalization system under study.

Personalized services hold enormous appeal for users as they offer seamless access to a wide set of resources available in/accessible through the library. Creating personalized customer services is hence essential for the survival of service institutions. In the context of libraries, personalization is projected as the next biggest challenge after digital libraries. Libraries and library professionals accord utmost preference to selective search and retrieval of information resources since at the organization stage itself, the library merges the individual requests gathered for collection development or access management and again at the time of service, these diverse interests are to be effectively identified. In the context of higher education and research, especially in the disciplines of science and technology, the efficacy of subject retrieval is time tested. Any attempt to improve the quality of subject terms used in the personalization system thus enhances the utility of the system as well retrieval precision. Libraries need to look for various sources to collect standard terms relevant to users' subject interests. These are to be then suitably related, carefully linked and functionally merged into a subject term control and assignment system. Though challenging, this task is crucial for the ultimate success and propagation of personalization systems. As an illustration, standardized subject terms for two important disciplines, Computer Science and Physics, are presented in detail below.

## 5.2. STANDARDIZED TERMS FOR COMPUTER SCIENCE AND PHYSICS

To indicate the level of standardization achieved, a brief discussion of the standardization achieved for Computer Science is presented below. With the aid of subject terms gathered from the specializations of the 34 Special Interest Groups (SIGs) of ACM [**ACM**] and the research areas [**CSE**], courses [**CSE1**] and projects [**CSE2**] of faculty members in these departments, standardized representation of subject terms for researchers in computer and allied disciplines and those having computer related specializations in other branches has been attempted, as shown in table 5.1. Similarly, to determine standard subject terms in Physics, INSPEC thesauri could have been the obvious choice. The requirement was not for very exhaustive subject terms but rather standard terms to represent subject specializations of the Institute's researchers. Thus the personalization system employed alternate but credible sources like special chapters or special interest groups of scientific and engineering societies, freely available classification schemes like Physics and Astronomy Classification Scheme [**PACS**], course headings followed by renowned universities etc. In the background of the subject areas listed [**PHY**] and by using the PACS, similar categorization has been attempted for specializations in Physics.

*Table 5.1: Standard Subject Terms for Computer Science*

| ***Broad Term*** | ***Narrow Terms*** |
|---|---|
| Computation Theory/ Theoretical Computer Science | Complexity theory, parallel computation, computational geometry, number theory, graph theory, distributed computation, distributed processing, parallel processing, mathematical modeling, computational problem solving, symbolic manipulation, algebraic manipulation, mathematical |

| | |
|---|---|
| | computation, symbolic computation, data structures, simulation, modeling, cybernetics, genetic optimization, geometric modeling, high level synthesis, real time systems, number theoretic computation, algebraic computation, computational complexity, switching theory, logic design, discrete structures, automata theory, optimization techniques, operations research, computational structure, numerical analysis, chaos, fractals, dynamical systems, formal systems, fuzzy sets, queuing theory, state event systems |
| VLSI Design | VLSI CAD, VLSI circuits and systems, VLSI design, VLSI testing |
| Algorithms | Algorithm design, algorithm analysis, parallel algorithms |
| Bioinformatics | Computational biology |
| Programming Language | Formal languages, concepts, tools, design, implementation, use, specific programming languages-Ada, APL, C, OOP, visual programming |
| Software Engineering | Process improvement, software development, CASE, object-oriented methods, software maintenance, software testing, fault tolerance, formal verification, system software, application software, software reliability |
| Applied Computing | Experimental computing, strategic research, computing management, technology transfer |
| Computer Architecture | Computer organization, computer design, hardware. hardware circuits, microprocessor. electrical circuits, linear circuits, pulse circuits, digital circuits, systems programming, instrumentation, modern microprocessors, optical electronics, hardware reliability, groupware |

| | |
|---|---|
| Compiler Design | Compiler design, memory compiler |
| Artificial Intelligence | Expert systems, decision support systems, machine learning, knowledge based systems, intelligent information systems, logic, logic programming, pattern recognition, machine intelligence, intelligent systems, knowledge acquisition, classifier learning, intelligent agents, digital circuit reasoning, speech synthesis, combinatorial optimization, knowledge discovery |
| Embedded Systems | Design technology, hardware frameworks, software solutions |
| Computers - Physically Handicapped | Handicapped, physical disabilities, disability solutions |
| Computers - Society | Ethics, societal concerns, social impact, internet privacy |
| Computer-Human Interaction | Interaction process, user interface |
| Data Communication/ Computer Networks | Network architecture, network protocols, distributed systems, interconnection networks, LANs, telematics, telemedicine |
| Computer Science/IT Education | Curricula, courses, syllabi, laboratories, teaching, pedagogy, software education |
| Design Automation | Electronic design automation, computer-aided design, computer-aided testing, industrial electronics, manufacturing systems, optical electronics, robotics |
| Documentation | Online help systems, user manual, user support |
| Electronic Commerce | Payment systems |
| Computer Graphics | Image processing, robust geometric computing, exact geometric computing, digital image processing, digital signal processing, computer vision, medical imaging |
| Information Retrieval | Information storage, retrieval, dissemination, search engines, text analysis, information systems design, |

| | |
|---|---|
| | information processing, information theory, coding techniques, text processing |
| Measurement and Evaluation | System performance, evaluation tools |
| Microarchitecture | Instruction-level parallelism, microarchitects, microprogrammers, superscalar, computer microarchitecture, pipelined, MIMD computer architecture |
| Management Information Systems | Business information technology |
| Multimedia | Multimedia computing, multimedia communication, multimedia systems, multimedia storage, multimedia applications |
| Mobile computing | Portable computers, wireless networks, nomadic computing, mobile user services, mobile networking, mobile agents, mobile communication, mobile ad hoc networks |
| Data management | Database systems, database technology, database management systems, database engineering |
| Operating Systems | OS design |
| Security | Computer security, communications security, protection, firewall, encryption, decryption, cryptographic protocols, cryptography |
| Internet | Web, Hypertext, Hypermedia, Internet protocols, TCP/IP |

*Table 5.2: Standard Subject Terms for Physics*

| ***Broad Term*** | ***Narrow Terms*** |
|---|---|
| Astrophysics | Nuclear astrophysics, elementary particle processes, atomic processes, atomic interactions, molecular processes, molecular interactions, chemical processes, chemical interactions, polarization, scattering, atomic spectra, molecular spectra, hydrodynamics, magnetohydro- |

| | |
|---|---|
| | dynamics, plasmas, relativity, gravitation, thermodynamic processes, dust processes, dark matter, cosmic rays, interplanetary space, solar physics, stellar characteristics, stellar properties, interstellar, galaxies, extragalactic, cosmology |
| Atmospheric Physics | Atmospheric turbulence, atmospheric gases, spectral absorption, crystal phenomena, aerosols, air pollution, scattering, polarization, image transmission, image formation, remote sensing, LIDAR, atmospheric sound, atmospheric electricity, atmospheric effects, meteorology, gravity waves, boundary layer, ionic interactions, cloud physics, climatology, weather, climate dynamics |
| Atomic Physics | Electronic structure, electronic transitions, electronic binding, mathematical calculations, electron correlation, electronic structure, atomic properties, atomic masses, mass spectra, abundances, isotopes, electric moments, magnetic moments, atomic spectra, fluorescence, phosphorescence, Zeeman effect, Stark effect, photon interactions |
| Biomedical Optics & Optical Imaging | Biomedical engineering, biochemical engineering, biomedical optics, image processing, medical imaging, tomography, image reconstruction, pattern recognition, laser imaging, image analysis |
| Condensed Matter Physics | X-ray diffraction, x-ray scattering, neutron diffraction, neutron scattering, electron diffraction, electron scattering, liquid crystals, crystallography, crystal defects, dislocations, radiation damage, mechanical properties, acoustical properties, lattice dynamics, phonons, phase equilibria, phase transitions, thermal properties, transport properties, |

| | |
|---|---|
| | quantum tunneling, quantum fluids, quantum solids, thin films, electronic structure, disordered solids, liquid metals, semiconductors, electronic transitions, electronic transport, insulators, conductivity, photons, photovoltaic effects, photoconduction, acoustoelectric, excitons, magnetoacoustic, electron states, surface conductivity, quantum Hall effect, superconductivity, magnetic properties, diamagnetism, paramagnetism, superparamagnetism, magnetic resonance, Mossbauer effect, electron paramagnetic resonance, nuclear magnetic resonance, dielectrics, piezoelectrics, ferroelectrics, optical properties, photoluminescence, electron emission, ion emission |
| Educational Physics | Course design, course evaluation, Physics education, curricula, teaching methods, teacher training |
| Electrodynamics | Quantum electrodynamics, cavity quantum electrodynamics, micromasers, specific calculations, experimental tests |
| Experimental Nuclear Physics | Storage rings, betatrons, accelerators, cyclotrons, synchrotrons, particle sources and targets, electron sources, neutron sources, ion sources, polarized targets, beam handling, charged particle spectrometers, spectroscopy, radiation detectors, computer interfaces, computer data analysis |
| Ferroelectricity | Ferroelectricity, antiferroelectricity, curie point, phase transitions, domain structure, hysteresis, switching phenomena, ferroelectric materials, ferroelectrics, |
| Fiber Optics | Fiber optics, fabrication, cladding, testing, fiber testing, fiber parameters, propagation, scattering, losses, solitons, birefringence, polarization, gradient- |

| | |
|---|---|
| | index, sensors, gyros, fiber waveguides, couplers, arrays, fiber networks, optical networks, fiber-optical devices |
| Fiber & Integrated Optics | Integrated optical systems, fabrication techniques, lithography, pattern transfer, interconnects, holographic interconnects, waveguides, couplers, arrays, hybrid systems |
| Group Theory | Groups, classical groups, Lie groups-general properties, structure and representation, discrete subgroups, Lie algebras, infinite-dimensional Lie groups, quantum groups, nuclear models |
| Laser Physics | Resonators, cavities, amplifiers, arrays, rings, modulation, tuning, mode locking, Q-switching, beam characteristics, applications, laser spectroscopy, free-electron lasers, laser-driven accelerators, laser-plasma interactions, laser Doppler velocimeters, laser ablation, laser-beam impact phenomena, laser beams, laser radiation, laser deposition, laser diodes, laser imaging, laser cooling |
| Lasers & Non-linear Optics | Optical susceptibility, hyper polarizability, stimulated Raman scattering, CARS, phase conjugation, photorefractive and Kerr effects, beam trapping, self-focusing and defocusing, self-phase modulation, frequency conversion, harmonic generation, parametric down conversion, entangled photons, optical bistability, multistability, switching, optical pulse generation, pulse compression, nonlinear optical systems, optical instabilities, optical chaos, optical spatio-temporal dynamics, optical solitons, nonlinear guided waves, optical parametric oscillators and amplifiers |
| Liquid Crystals | Molecular and microscopic models, liquid crystal structure theory, smectic, nematic, cholesteric, orientational order, |

| | |
|---|---|
| | electric and magnetic field effects, surface phenomena, alignment, anchoring, anchoring transitions, surface-induced layering, surface-induced ordering, wetting, prewetting transitions, wetting transitions, defects, blue phases, defect-phases, micro confined, droplets, cylinders, randomly confined, polymer dispersed, porous systems, lyotropic systems, polymer liquid crystals, transitions |
| Magnetic Materials | Saturation moments, magnetic susceptibilities, spin waves, exchange and superexchange interactions, spin-density waves, magnetic anisotropy, magnetic impurity interactions, magnetic phase boundaries, magnetic transitions, metamagnetism, valence fluctuation, Kondo lattice, heavy-fermion phenomena, magnetocaloric effect, magnetic cooling, spin crossover, giant magnetoresistance, ferromagnetic materials, antiferromagnetics, ferrimagnetics, amorphous and quasicrystalline, spin glasses, random magnets, magnetic liquids, magnetic semiconductors, magnetic recording materials. fine-particle systems, nanocrystalline materials, high coercivity materials, permanent magnets, molecular magnets, domain effects, magnetization curves, hysteresis, magnetic aftereffects, magnetic annealing, magnetostriction, magnetic resonances, Mossbauer effect |
| Mathematical Physics | Logic, set theory, algebra, knot theory, matrix theory, group theory, function theory, analysis, Fourier analysis, bifurcation theory, harmonic analysis, geometry, differential geometry, topology, probability theory, stochastic processes, Markov processes, decision |

| | |
|---|---|
| | theory, game theory, multivariate analysis, Monte Carlo studies, numerical approximation, numerical analysis, computational techniques, finite-difference methods, finite-element methods, spectral methods, collocation methods, symbolic computation |
| Molecular Physics | Molecular properties, molecular conformation, molecular symmetry, stereochemistry, interatomic distances, bond strengths, dissociation energies, barrier heights, rotational isomerism, electric and magnetic moments, polarizability, magnetic susceptibility, rotation, vibration, vibration-rotation constants, fine and hyperfine structure, ionization potentials, electron affinities, molecular core binding energy, mass spectra, correlation times, molecular spectra, nuclear resonance and relaxation, electron resonance and relaxation, multiple resonance, Mossbauer spectra, fluorescence and phosphorescence, radiationless transitions, quenching, optical activity, dichroism, Zeeman effect, Stark effect, magnetooptical effects, electrooptical effects, photoelectron spectra, oscillator and band strengths, transition moments, Frank-Condon factors, level crossing, optical pumping, autoionization, photoionization, diffuse spectra, predissociation, photodissociation, optical cooling, trapping, Rydberg states, multiphoton processes, intermolecular and atom-molecule potentials and forces, intramolecular energy transfer, intramolecular dynamics, ven der Waals molecules, electronic excitation and ionization of molecules, intermediate molecular states, molecular beams, charge transfer, electron scattering, positron scattering, |

| | |
|---|---|
| | exotic molecules, muonic molecules, mesonic molecules, hyperonic molecules, macromolecules, polymer molecules, molecular clusters, |
| Nonlinear Instabilities | Hydrodynamic instability, nonlinearity, bifurcation theory, secondary instability, interfacial instability, receptivity, chaotic phenomena |
| Nuclear Physics | Nuclear structure, properties of nuclei, nuclear energy levels, nuclear forces, few-body systems, nuclear models, nuclear matter, hypernuclei, radioactive decay, inbeam spectroscopy, electromagnetic transitions, proton emission, heavy particle decay, nuclear reactions, resonance reactions, direct reactions, fluctuation phenomena, polarization phenomena, quarks, gluons, QCD, relativistic heavy-ion collisions, meson and hyperon induced reactions, fission reactions, nuclear astrophysics, neutron physics, fission reactors, fusion reactors, isotope separation and enrichment, nuclear explosions, particle accelerators, spectrometers, spectroscopy, radiation detectors |
| Particle Physics | Field theory, gauge field theory, strings and branches, symmetry and conservation laws, S-matrix theory, relativistic scattering theory, unified field theory. electroweak interactions, quantum electrodynamics, quantum chromodynamics, phenomenological quark models, neutrino interactions. leptonic, semileptonic, and radiative decays of mesons, baryons, bosons, hadrons,, lepton-lepton interactions, polarization, quarks, gauge bosons, magnetic monopoles, axions |
| Photoelectron Spectroscopy | Ultraviolet, vacuum ultraviolet, X-ray |
| Polymers | Plastics, rubber, synthetic fibers. natural |

| | |
|---|---|
| | fibers, reinforced polymers, polymer based composites, conducting polymers, nonlinear optics with polymers, polymers on surfaces, adhesion, copolymers, phase transitions, structure, nanoparticles, biopolymers, polyelectrolytes, thermosetting polymers, associated polymers, polymer solutions, polymer blends, polymer melts, block copolymers, elastomeric polymers, |
| Quantum Chaos | Semiclassical methods, numerical simulations of chaotic systems, communication using chaos |
| Quantum Theory | Quantum mechanics, solutions of wave equations, relativistic wave equations, field theory, matter waves, Bose-Einstein Condensation, Fermi gases |
| Relativity | General relativity, approximation methods, numerical relativity, post Newtonian approximation, perturbation theory, gravitational waves, self gravitating systems, relativistic stars, Einstein-Maxwell spacetimes, Kaluza-Klein theory, unified field theories, quantum gravity, quantum field theory, supergravity, black holes, gravitational wave detectors, |
| Semiconductors | Elemental defect levels. III-V semiconductors, II-VI semiconductors, amorphous semiconductors. metallic glasses, organic semiconductors, inorganic semiconductors, liquid semiconductors, spin polarized transport, magnetic semiconductors |
| Sensors | Chemical, optical, electrical, movement, gas, electrochemical |
| Superconductivity | Phenomenological theories (two-fluid, Ginzburg-Landau), BCS theory, spin fluctuations, polarons, bipolarons, resonating valence bond model, anyon |

| | |
|---|---|
| | mechanism, marginal Fermi liquid, Luttinger liquid, pairing symmetries, type I and type II superconductors, thermodynamic properties, superconductivity phase diagrams, transport properties (electric and thermai conductivity, thermoelectric effects), optical properties, magnetic properties, electronic structure, phonons, mechanical properties, acoustical properties, fluctuations, proximity effects, tunneling phenomena, Josephson effects, transition temperature variations, superconducting materials, ruthenates, heavy-fermion superconductors, fullerenes, cuprate superconductors, superconducting films, multilayers, superlattices, heterostructures, mesoscopic systems, nanoscale systems, inhomogeneous superconductors, granular superconductors, composite superconductors, Josephson junction arrays, |
| Surface Science | Atomic, molecular, and ion beam impact and interactions with surfaces, surface treatments, passivation, surface hardening, adhesion, polymers on surfaces, surface structure, surface chemistry, microscopy |
| Thermoelectricity | Thermoelectric effects, thermoelectric transport, thermoelectric devices |
| Thin Films | Liquid thin films, structure and morphology, physical properties, electronic transport phenomena, electrical properties, magnetic properties, dielectric thin films |
| Waste Utilization | Radioactive wastes, waste disposal |
| X-ray Crystallography | X-ray diffraction and scattering, X-ray absorption spectroscopy, EXAFS, NEXAFS, XANES, X-ray reflectometry |

## 5.3. INTERFACING STANDARDIZED TERMS INTO THE PERSONALIZATION SYSTEM

The database table for the subject term assignment contains a subject code, broad term and narrower terms, and the user can enable or disable narrower terms under a broad term. In the event of the user opting only for a narrower term, s/he may be intimated about other related terms for inclusion. Whenever a new term not stored in the database is suggested, it will be checked for synonyms, and if not at all present, will be added appropriately under a relevant broad term. If no suitable entries are available, it will be added as a new broad term. Presently this is done manually since it involves decision-making and requires consultation with subject experts. However, once the database is populated with terms beyond a certain threshold, term relations could be built into the system so that the system itself makes suitable choices about ordering and simultaneous occurrence of terms to the desired extent. A similar strategy has been adopted for other departments as well. The subject terms arrived at for different departments are merged into one database table to further information support for interdisciplinary and cross specialization aspects, so common in technology research. In the next chapter, we discuss about the design and implementation of the personalization system, undertaken with the experience gathered in the subject matter of discussion of earlier chapters.

## REFERENCES

1. **ACM** Special Interest Groups Guide. http://www.acm.org/sigs/guide98.html
2. **CSE.** Research Areas, Dept of Computer Science & Engineering, Indian Institute of Technology, Kharagpur. http://www.iitkgp.ernet.in/departments/research.php?deptcode=CS
3. **CSE1**. Courses, Dept of Computer Science & Engineering, Indian Institute of Technology, Kharagpur. http://www.iitkgp.ernet.in/~cse/courses.html

4. **CSE2**. Research Projects, Dept of Computer Science & Engineering, Indian Institute of Technology, Kharagpur. http://www.iitkgp.ernet.in/~cse/researchmain.html

5. **PACS.** Physics and Astronomy Classification Scheme. prepared by the American Institute of Physics (AIP) in collaboration with certain other members of the International Council on Scientific and Technical Information (ICSTI). http://www.aip.org/pacs/

6. **PHY.** Research Areas, Dept of Physics & Meteorology, Indian Institute of Technology, Kharagpur. http://www.iitkgp.ernet.in/departments/home.php?Deptcode=MP

# Chapter 6
# Design and Implementation of Library Personalization System

## 6.0. INTRODUCTION

The feasibility of this project had been accurately assessed from the genuine interest expressed by most of the libraries who responded to the questionnaire (see results of the questionnaire study in chapter 3) regarding adoption of suitable tools and techniques for user centred information services. The previous chapters highlighted the need and viability of creating an integrated user interest management system and creating profiles using standardized terms. IIT Libraries are strong in electronic content and computer and communication infrastructure to manipulate personalized delivery of research information to individual researchers. The current chapter discusses the actual design and implementation of personalized information delivery, 'A Personalized Selective Access Information System (SAI)' catering to higher education and state of the art research at the Central Library of Indian Institute of Technology Kharagpur, the model used in the study.

## 6.1. SYSTEM DESIGN

The new system must be designed based on user requirements and detailed analysis. This phase of system designing is most crucial in the development of a system. The major emphasis of a software design is to effectively break down a large problem into manageable parts. This systematic decomposition of the problem to handle complexity is the essence of good software design. Normally, the system design proceeds in two stages:

***Preliminary or general design***: In the preliminary or general design, the features of the new system are specified. The costs of implementing these features and the benefits to be derived are estimated. If the project is still considered to be feasible, we move on to the detailed design stage.

***Structure or Detailed design***: In the detailed design stage, computer oriented work begins in earnest. At this stage, the design of the system becomes more structured. Structure design is a blue print of a computer system solution to a given problem having the same components and inter-relationship among the components as the original problem. Input, output and processing specifications are drawn up in detail. In the design stage, the programming language and the platform in which the new system will run are also decided upon.

### 6.1.1. Statement of the Problem

In the postal network, all letters meant for the local post office arrive from different regions, zones and places, are shuffled together and sent by the post office higher in the hierarchy. Once they reach the local post office, the letters are further sorted according to the postmen covering different beats who again sort the letters as per their convenience in distributing based on the easiest and shortest path to follow. Similarly, in all service networks, some sort of assembling and de-assembling takes place to deliver the most efficient service possible, subject to the different constraints. In a library setting, different users make recommendations for buying books, subscribing journals, licensing electronic resources, availing ILL/DDS facilities etc., and the library then proceeds with satisfying these varied requirements by cumulating requests of a particular type such as requisitions for new books. Once these materials/services are made available to users, the library has to again establish connection with the right user for the right resource. Such a connection, unthinkable in the paper domain, has been made possible in the electronic scenario due to the advantages of computer-aided information processing tools and technologies, especially after the evolution of web technology aided database tools. Through personalization, the librarian attempts to slice the library according to the interests of individual users so that every user will be able to effectively utilize the resources and services which s/he requires the most.

### 6.1.2. Feasibility Study

Faculty members and researchers are so engrossed in teaching and research activities that they hardly get enough time to visit the Library and browse its resources to identify the relevant ones. The availability of electronic information in networks has made it possible to effectively match these resources as per the subject specializations and content usage of individual researchers and deliver highly specialized and relevant resources through email/web links. Successful implementation of 'mylibrary' projects in several libraries in the developed world and similar practices by web portals demonstrated the feasibility of such an implementation in an academic institute like the IIT characterized by superior computer and communication infrastructure, sufficient amount of electronic resources and a highly demanding and ever serious user base.

### 6.1.3. Requirements Analysis and Specification

The primary objective of the requirements analysis and specification phase is to carefully understand and correctly document the actual requirements of the customer, in this context the library and its clientele. In the requirements gathering subtask, the design team collects all the relevant information from the customer regarding the software product to be developed. Incomplete and inconsistent (those which contradicts some other existing) requirements are eliminated altogether. After all the ambiguities, inconsistencies and incompleteness have been resolved, and the requirement properly understood, the requirements specification is worked out.

### *6.1.3.1. Production Functions Overview*

Besides there being several web search engines, electronic resources accessed through printed subscriptions and as part of the INDEST consortium are now also being accessed through the web. Due to heavy traffic or increase in pages to be displayed, coupled with less time for researchers to search these portals, the search results retrieved may contain records irrelevant to users' preferences. This may also lead to under use of these resources, consequently keeping the researchers ill-informed of the latest developments in their chosen areas of specialization. To address these problems, the content personalization initiative must use both database and web technology, aiming to optimize relevant results. The system should also act as a single window system to collect, organize and manage electronic resources of interest to researchers through personal web pages on the server. They may also augment these pages with suitable links to their own publications, using these sites to communicate with students, colleagues and peers in the concerned field to create virtual communities or invisible colleges of specialized research, so that the impact and benefits of specialized research may further be directed towards potential users. Satisfied researchers may put to increased effect productive use of these resources, leading to efficient use of both research information and the researchers' time for more fruitful research tasks.

In this study, an attempt has been made to describe both the external requirements as well as the system interfaces for the proposed content personalization system for IIT Kharagpur. This may act as a guide for use by the developers and form the basis for validating the final delivered system. Any future changes made in the requirements will have to undergo a formal change approval process. Further, the developer would be responsible for asking for clarifications, wherever necessary, and will not make any alterations without the permission of the client. The developer would thus be responsible for

a. Developing the system
b. Installing the software on clients' hardware
c. Conducting any user training that might be needed for effectively using the system, and
d. Maintaining the system for a period of one year after installation.

#### *6.1.3.2. User Characteristics*

The main users of this system will comprise the teaching faculty of IIT Kharagpur, who are conversant with computers and programs such as web browsers, editors and text processors.

#### *6.1.3.3. External Interface Requirements*

**User Interface:** The project address should be given in the browser which then displays the login page

### 6.1.4. Design

#### *6.1.4.1. Software Constraints:*

**Server:** The server needs multi user operating system due to security and real time operations in a distributed fashion supporting multiple users. Due to cost considerations, this system has been implemented using Linux operating system.

**Client:** Web browser on a PC or thin client

#### *6.1.4.2. Hardware Constraints:*

**Server:** The system will run on Intel Xeon machine with 2064 MB RAM

**Client:** PC or thin client with network connection

#### *6.1.4.3. Acceptance Criteria*

Before accepting the system, the developer must demonstrate how the system works. The developer must also make sure through test cases that all necessary conditions are satisfied.

### *6.1.4.4. Data Flow Diagrams:*

Context Diagram:

Level 0

This figure shows the system at its top level where a user can access his/her web page by providing the specific username and password. In case of a mismatch in this data, an error message is flashed and the user is prompted the login screen again to re-enter the data correctly. If the login and password are found correct, the links to different resources selectively retrieved by the system such as books, journals, news, search engines, web links etc. may be viewed. A new user can also register with the system by filling up the registration form.

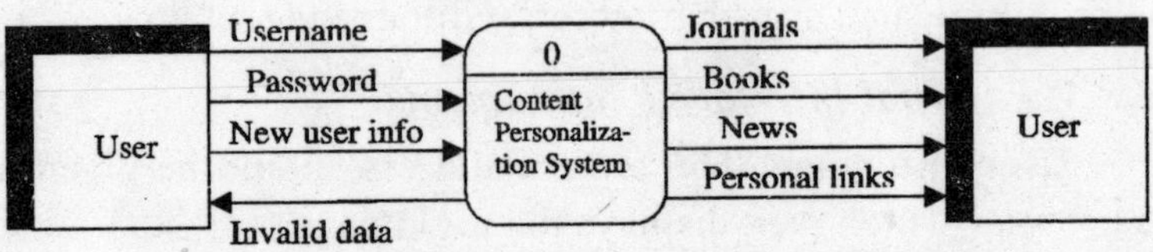


**Fig. 6.1: Context Level Data Flow Diagram (Level 0)**

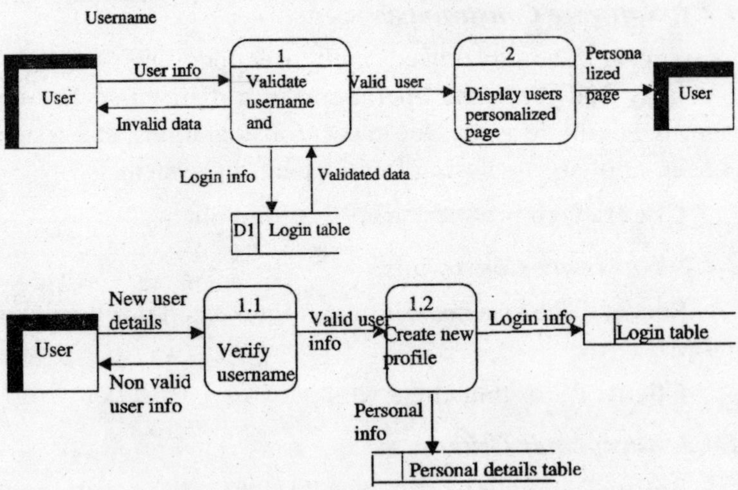


**Fig. 6.2: Data Flow Diagram (Level 1)**

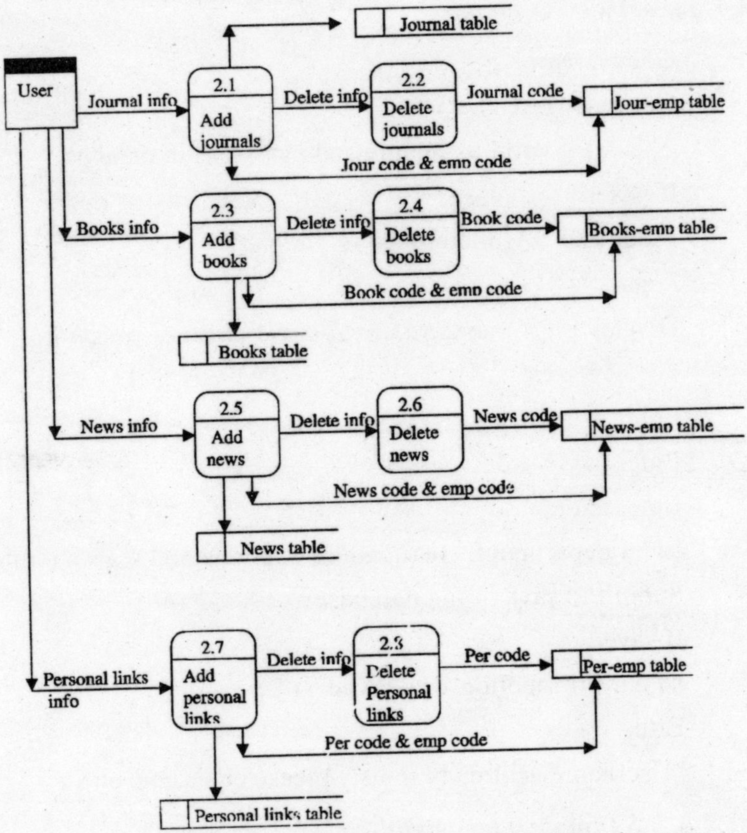


**Fig. 6.3: Data Flow Diagram (Level 2)**

## *6.1.4.5. Structure Charts*

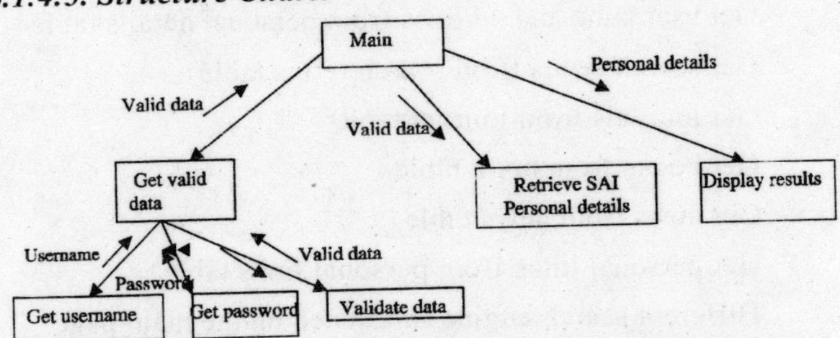


**Fig. 6.4: Structure Chart of Personalization System**

#### *6.1.4.6. Modules*

*6.1.4.6.1. Login module:*

Get username

Get password

Check for valid username and password in database

If yes

Enter into SAI main page

Else

Display error message 'Invalid username or password'

For new user

Enter username

Enter password

Enter name

Enter department, email, address, phone no., search terms

Submit to save in the database

If saved

"Your information was saved"

Else

"Username is already in use, please enter new one".

*6.1.4.6.2. SAI main page module:*

Connect to SAI database

Check for valid username and password

Get username and address from personal details table

Get search terms from search terms table

Get journals from journal table

Get books from book table

Get news from news table

Get personal links from personal links table

Different search engines are listed on the main page.

Search terms and search engine of user's interest will be selected to get search results.

Search results are displayed on a new window.

*6.1.4.6.3. Add and delete modules:*

In this module, we can add and delete journals, books, news and personal links.

Connect to SAI database

If delete journals, books, news, personal links

Delete the above items from the particular user's record.

Else

If add

Case journals:

Check whether journal code exists in journal-emp table

If yes

Then

Display "journal already exists "

Else check whether journal code exits in journal table

If yes

add journal code, and empcode to journal-emp table

else

add journal code, journal address and journal name to journal table

add Journal code and empcode in journal-emp table

Case books:

Check whether book code exists in book-emp table

If yes

Then

Display "book already exists"

Else check whether book code exits in books table

If yes

add book code, and empcode to book-emp table

else

add book code, book address and book name to books table

add book code and empcode in book-emp table

Case news:

Check whether news code exists in news-emp table

If yes

Then

Display “news already exists “

Else check whether news code exits in news table

If yes

add news code, and empcode to news-emp table

else

add news code, news address and news name to news table

add news code and empcode in news_emp table

Case personal links:

Check whether personal code exists in per-emp table

If yes

Then

Display “link already exists “

Else check whether personal code exits in personal table

If yes

add personal code, and empcode to per-emp table

else

add personal code, personal address and personal name to personal table

add Personal code and empcode in per_emp table

*6.1.4.6.4. Add and delete search terms module:*

In this module search terms are added and/or deleted

Connect to SAI database

If add search terms

Search terms will be added into particular user's record

Else delete

Selected search term was deleted from her/his record.

## 6.2. SYSTEM IMPLEMENTATION

The Central Library, IIT Kharagpur is among the pioneers in adopting the latest computer and information technology tools for providing client-centred electronic information services in the country, aided as it is by an extremely rich and unique collection of e-journals, e-books, bibliographic/full text electronic databases in stand-alone format or via networked CD/through web access and so on. Due to publishers' print/electronic plus policies, the Library has been able to successfully access electronic versions of new files. This has received a further boost due to the Ministry of Human Resources Development's (MHRD's) Indian National Digital Library in Engineering Science and Technology (INDEST) consortium, enabling subscription to full-text electronic resources and bibliographic databases for 38 leading engineering and technological institutions in the country including the IITs (7), IISc (1), NITs / RECs (17), IIMs (6) and a few other institutions directly funded by the MHRD [**Arora** and **Agrawal**]. As a result of this initiative, the full text e-journals in IIT Kharagpur have increased more than 8 fold from 600 journals in 2000 to 5381 journals in 2003.

Apart from arranging a few important bibliographic and full text databases on standalone and networked modes in its Electronic Library, the Central Library has also offered an Electronic Selective Dissemination of Information (E-SDI) service for faculty members, using some of the frequently updated bibliographic electronic databases. The strategy consists of preparing profiles of faculty members based on their subject specializations, searching these profiles vis-a-vis latest updates of the database, and sending the bibliographic information to the concerned faculty members through email. The difficulty in making the E-SDI service automated due to the proprietary software used, the constraints in offering full text of retrieved references since many journals were not subscribed by the Library or by other libraries with which it had collaborative ILL/DDS arrangements, and the spread of web access of journals etc. forced the Library to modify this service and transform it into a personalization service, utilizing the current proliferation of electronic resources and emerging web technology. MHRD's support for a research project, 'A Personalized Selective Access Information System (SAI)' in 2003 with a grant of Rs. 8 lakhs has helped the library concentrate more productively on implementing a suitable personalization system for IIT Kharagpur and for possible extension to libraries of the other IITs.

### 6.2.1. Steps in Personalization

As has been spelt out in Chapter 1, the personalization system is to be implemented as described in the following steps:

**Step 1:** Configuring a Linux based web server for content personalization with local hosting of INDEST contents is the first step in proceeding with this initiative. Since local hosting is not considered in the first step of INDEST activity, the personalization server should work with/without locally hosted bibliographic/table of contents data and seek contents as and when needed from the distributed publisher web servers. This requires incorporation of a personalization server as an intermediary before interaction between the institute gateway and publishers' sites. The performance of the personalization system depends on many technical and operational overheads.

**Step 2:** Web pages incorporating user details and their fields of interest are to be created for the Institute's faculty, scientific and research staff. These pages should be created with the active participation of the users so that they feel sufficiently involved in the process. This may also help to correctly map the crucial item of subject specialization of the individual concerned.

The personalization server will be intelligent and capable enough to continuously monitor the use patterns at an individual user level. It may start with user profiles entered and modified by user/information intermediary through web forms. The server must also use the content caching and cookies stored in the Institute gateway to monitor the status of information usage and to identify frequently used contents. Personalization identifies the visitor using a cookie or session logon and dynamically generates a page specific to the visitor, which is not cached at proxy servers and most server caches.

**Step 3:** The search engine performs the task of matching and generating the matched contents. The matched contents with links to full text are hosted in their web pages in the personalization server or sent as email alerts. Since all the IITs make use of fiber optic ATM Intranet, the links can be easily downloaded by users after perusing the results sent through email/ kept on the personalization site.

**Step 4:** Feedback and Profile Modification. This step is vital as it would provide inputs about the utility of the results generated by the Personalization System and constructively guide the system to modify the user profiles. This step may also act as an indirect evaluation of the personalized information service.

### 6.2.2. System Components

The MyLibrary projects mentioned earlier follow similar strategies for implementing a personalized library system. There are commercial recommender systems available for managing customer integrated enterprises such as E-piphany (see http:// www.epiphany. com/ for details) and BlueMartini (http:// www.bluemartini.com) which a library may buy. Alternatively, libraries can create their own solutions. MyLibrary software is available for free download at http://dewey.library.nd.edu/ mylibrary/download/.

#### *6.2.2.1. Content Serving System*

Electronic resources are made accessible through campus

LAN from publishers'/providers' servers as part of subscription to printed counterparts and through INDEST consortium. Apart from this, electronic resources, databases, electronic supplements of printed books available in local LAN, higher education resources available on the Internet and portals as well as search engines on the web are also incorporated as pools of content to serve the immediate information requirements of Institute researchers and faculty members.

#### *6.2.2.2. User Interest Management System*

The profiles developed earlier for the Electronic SDI are suitably modified and augmented with additional information from the home pages of faculty members and other sources **[Annual Report, A Profile of Research and Development at IIT Kharagpur, Research and Development Handbook-1996]** available in the Institute.

#### *6.2.2.3. Search Engine*

Most of the resources being provided with native search engines, it is extremely difficult to bypass these due to the restrictions imposed by the database providers because of the commercial interests involved. Licensing rights as part of consortium and access rights through subscriptions permit only selective search and access of few records and hence it is beyond the permissible rights of the Library to copy entire records into the local servers for working with the search engine developed locally. Thus to work with these constraints, the search engine presently developed contains the following features:

1) Users need not retype search parameters in the different search interfaces offered by web links of different service providers
2) Search terms entered may be redirected automatically to the native search engine of the selected resource, saving user time and effort

#### *6.2.2.4. Personalized Content Delivery*

Being aware of the benefits and limitations of the 'push' technology of email while operating the Electronic SDI, it was decided to go for the pull approach of keeping retrieved results with their web links in the personalized pages of faculty members. However, whenever a page is refreshed with new records, a general alert can be sent through email, stating the updation of their personalized page.

The system developed for personalizing electronic resources for the faculty and researchers of the Institute consists of the following basic components:

* Web server to host service using web tools
* Database engine like MySQL to collect and manipulate user interests
* PHP/java scripts to communicate between the database engine and the web server (client request)
* Web browser for client access

Resources can be selected using tick box by the user as per requirement. Users also can customize page layout as well as order and arrangement of personal links. The client browser must support cookies and must be configured to not look for content in its cache.

### 6.2.3. Working of the System

The user needs to login to the system with password (encrypted and stored in the database for online validation) to access his/her personalized page. The system has provisions to gather the subject interests of researchers from their websites and their ongoing interactions with the Library as well as the personalization system. There is further provision for the user to add/remove subject terms and access appropriate virtual links to the different services offered. These terms automatically scan the different online services and e-journals available to flash a list of information resources matching the search term. There is added provision for the user to select a term for a particular service (such as IEL online or ScienceDirect) or use more than one term on one service or a group of services. Apart from interfacing the locally available (full text and bibliographic databases, e-books) and network accessible electronic resources (e-journals and bibliographic/full text databases), the system also provides virtual links to the following:

* Free electronic journals available on the Internet
* Free e-books on the web
* News sites covering S&T as well as general information
* Academic information on the Internet such as websites of research and educational institutions
* Search engines and portals on the web

The user needs to simply configure the choices on the personalization page to achieve suitable results. Apart from the mere add/remove option, the user can also create fresh links and sub links reflecting his/her different requirements. The system also provides options for searching the library OPAC for getting information regarding the borrowing details and a web form to address queries to the librarian. A typical page in the system is shown in Figure 6.5.

### 6.2.4. System Features

The System allows users to search, collect and organize general web resources relating to their specific interests. It is thus a combination of manual decision rule system and content-based system. The System incorporates features enabling users to search the library database as well as the World Wide Web with more functionality, without expending much time and effort getting familiar with the intricacies of the various native search interfaces developed by different publishers and database providers. Another advantage of the System is that it offers users the ability to create personal web links, interact with the library, use a protection mechanism to access their data and have the web links checked and updated when they are not functioning.

This feature, when used efficiently, may lead to a single window system to collect, manipulate, use and manage electronic resources of interest to them, to disseminate information regarding their publications and also to participate in virtual research communities.

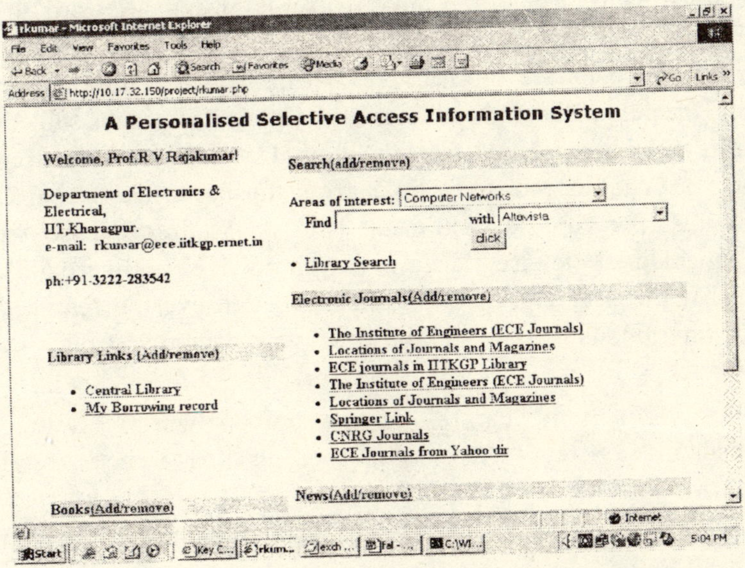


**Fig. 6.5: Screenshot of a Researcher's Personalized Page after Login with the Appropriate Password**

The experiences gained in operating the Electronic SDI Service and the feedback received helped to accurately analyze and successfully gather the information requirements of target users, especially in the context of alerting and updating research papers published in their areas of interest. A survey of the library personalization projects mentioned earlier, in particular the project at the University of North Carolina [**MyLibrary@NCState**], helped to identify additional features like patron information from library automation package, contacting library professionals for personalized queries etc.

As an initial step, the contact details of faculty members

in different departments of the Institute and their research interests are collected and stored in the database. URLs and subject specializations of e-journals, e-books and other research materials available on the web are also collected and stored in the database. When a particular user connects to the personalization web server through user login and password, the PHP (Hyper-text Preprocessor) embedded in the HTML connects to the user database and retrieves her/his personal information from the personal details table; areas of interests from the subject terms table; journal links from the journal table; books links from the books table and news links from the news table. Search engines like Google, Altavista, IEL, ACM Portal, Elsevier ScienceDirect etc. are placed in a drop down box (Figure 6.5), so that the user can quickly and easily retrieve the required information using any database or search engine from one window.

The salient features of the personalization system, Personalized Selective Access Information (SAI) System, are as follows:

After the initial login, the user is presented with a personal page (Figure 6.5), the content and links of which are based on his/her subject specialization.

1. **Welcome message** with his address, email and phone number.
2. **Search:** The user is provided with his areas of interest and multiple search engines. Just by clicking on his area of interest he can connect to the search engine of his choice and get quick results without explicitly typing the keyword(s).
3. **Library Links:** A link to the library is provided to check information regarding books borrowed, corresponding due dates, overdue charged and any other person centric queries from the Library housekeeping database system.
4. **E-journals and E-books:** The user is provided with links

to e-journals and e-books related to his areas of interest. S/he can also add any additional links related to e-journals and e-books of his choice in the add page. Further, a checkbox option is provided to delete links if a particular link is found to be irrelevant in satisfying the impending information needs (see figure 6.6).

5. **News Links:** The SAI design includes news links for users, which provide further links regarding upcoming worldwide conferences, science and technology magazines etc.
6. **Personal Links:** Facilitate addition of the links of users' personal interests.
7. **Ask a Librarian:** This link provides a facility to use the suggestion form of the library and to contact the Library Head/Section-in-charges.
8. **Protect Mechanism:** SAI utilizes a unique protection mechanism based on username and encrypted password through which only a registered user can login to view the personalized page.

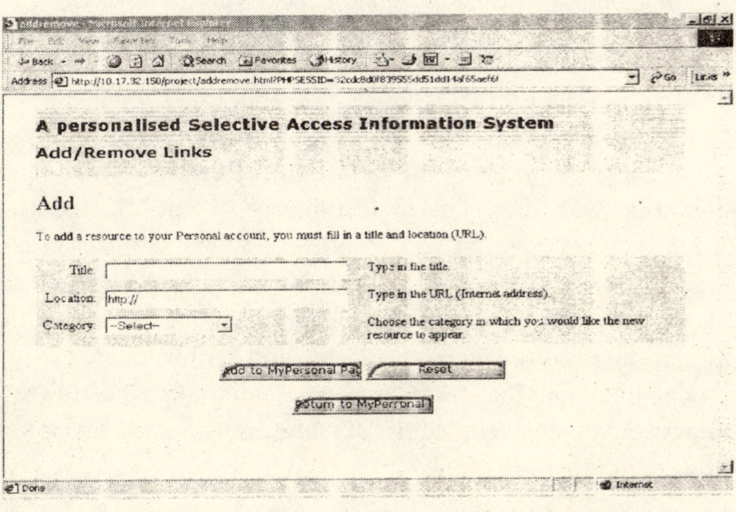


**Fig. 6.6: Add/Remove Link Feature in SAI**

### 6.2.5. System Architecture

The SAI system uses client-server architecture and has been implemented using PHP and Java script. The database used, MySQL, is an Open Source SQL database and the operating system is Linux. SAI services can be accessed through a web browser such as Internet Explorer or Netscape Navigator.

#### *6.2.5.1. Modules*

The system consists of several modules such as:

* **Login details:** Username and Password information.
* **Personal details:** Name, Department, Phone and Email-id.
* **Journals module:** Journal name and journal website address.
* **Books module:** Book name and http link to book site.
* **Subject terms module:** Terms related to users' areas of interest.
* **News module** and **Personal links module:** News with http links and user created links respectively.

#### *6.2.5.2. Tables*

Each of the journals, books, personal links, subject terms and news modules contain two tables. The master table of journal module contains information about journal code, journal name and journal web link. The child table represents the existing relation between journal and employee. When the user enters the information related to a journal, the existence of journal information in child table is checked and if it does not exist, the information is stored in both master and child tables. Books, personal links, subject terms and news modules also utilize a similar mechanism. Detailed list of tables used in implementation is presented in Annexure 2.

### 6.2.6. Proxy Level Use Data Collection

Unlike individual web servers that contain only limited

number of webpages, a proxy server situated in the middle-tier in the Internet infrastructure serves many web-clients and thus covers a wide scale of the web domain consisting of heterogeneous websites. Proxy caching can be used to reduce both the loading time of a webpage as well as the network traffic load at the server and client sides. The performance of proxy caches depends on their ability to predict future page requests correctly. Proxy traces may reveal the actual HTTP requests sent from multiple clients to multiple web servers. This may serve as a data source for characterizing the browsing behavior of a group of anonymous users sharing a common proxy server.

From the discussion above, it is evident that to perform research on general browsing behaviour, the log file data of a proxy server would be more appropriate because of the many-to-many relationship between sites and users. Log file data can offer valuable insight into website usage since it represents the activity of multiple users over a potentially long period of time compared to a limited number of users for an hour or two each. Based on this data user interests can be identified and collected through a proxy server, thus enriching the user interest identification in the SAI system.

In the SAI personalization implementation, locally copying all data of interest for personalized information retrieval is impossible; hence working with server side personalization will not lead to gathering any pertinent information about the user. There are additional limitations in client level personalization due to technical and administrative reasons. Thus the only way out is to implement proxy side personalization by configuring a proxy server to collect what happens at the client side with the personalization engine's retrieved results, involving user interaction of with the personalization system.

Every user being connected to a proxy server, as long as s/he does not change her/his installation settings, s/he will always log on to the same server. This implies that the log history of every user can always be found on the same server. Usually the

ISP does not make use of fixed IP-addresses, utilizing instead a pool of dynamic IP-addresses, which makes it more complicated to identify users. In IIT Kharagpur, since the machines used by users are in LAN, each user has a fixed IP-address.

For automatic profile generation and search result re-order, user browsing behaviour should be observed, based on which data user interests can be collected for new users and fine tuned for existing users. Web usage mining helps to collect information about user behavior and use patterns.

When a user accesses the SAI system, s/he is prompted to change the settings of the client machine's proxy to the SAI's proxy server, located in the Central Library so that the web usage data is collected from this proxy server's access log file. Here it is assumed that each user has a fixed IP address, consequently users are identified by their IP-addresses and unique user-ids. However, this study may fail to reveal the usage details if either more than one person uses one client machine or one person uses more than one client machine to access the personalized research results.

In the SAI system, proxy logs are used for clients' usage data, these logs being collected from the access log file of the proxy server. The data from the access log file is subsequently copied into a text file. Proxy log files are records of web server activity providing details about file requests to a web server as well as the server response to the requests. In the access log, which is the main log file, each line describes the source of a request, the file requested, the date and time of the request, the content type and length of the transferred file and other data such as errors and the identity of referring pages.

The following chapter discusses the testing of the system developed along with steps for collecting and implementing user feedback. Possible areas for improvement and the mechanism of system maintenance are also highlighted.

## REFERENCES

1. **Annual Report**. Indian Institute of Technology, Kharagpur. 1997-98, 1998-99, 1999-2000, 2000-2001, 2001-2002, and 2002-2003.
2. **A Profile of Research and Development at IIT Kharagpur**. Sponsored Research and Industrial Consultancy Cell. Indian Institute of Technology, Kharagpur. June 2003. p 171.
3. **Arora** (Jagdish) and **Agrawal** (Pawan). Indian Digital Library in Engineering Science and Technology (INDEST) Consortium: Consortia-Based Subscription to Electronic Resources for Technical Education System in India: A Government of India Initiative. International CALIBER 2003, Ahmedabad, 13-15 February 2003. In Proceedings Volume - Mapping Technology on Libraries and People. 2003. INFLIBNET Centre. Ahmedabad. p 271-290.
4. ***MyLibrary@NCState***. http://my.lib.ncsu.edu/
5. **Research and Development Handbook-1996**. Indian Institute of Technology, Kharagpur. November 1996. p 146.
6. **Websites** of IIT, Kharagpur (www.iitkgp.ernet.in/ www.iitkgp.ac.in) and of its different Departments/ Centres/Schools/Sections.

# Chapter 7

# Testing, Feedback, Improvement And Maintenance

## 7.0. INTRODUCTION

The personalization system developed in the last chapter is tested for its working and assessed to determine whether it has met all the requirements for which it was designed. The goal of testing is to ensure that the system designed and developed conforms to the requirements spelt out in the requirements specification. Feedback is more important in the client centred information support system like personalization due to the very fact that information professionals and researchers perceive and approach research information from different professional angles. Most of the time the researcher is more interested in identifying the most relevant article. On the other hand, the information professional would be mainly interested in notifying all relevant articles on the topic. This conflict of interests can best be bridged by a relevant feedback system which informs the system about the nature and type of literatures the researcher is interested in apart from results retrieved through term matching. The feedback provided by the user would definitely improve the working of the personalization system as also the quality of the results retrieved by it. It has been estimated that among the different steps of software development activity like feasibility study, requirements analysis and specification, system development, and testing and maintenance, the last one alone costs about 60% in terms of money and manpower. Maintenance is also important because the personalization system developed is being put to constant test, feedback and monitoring by library professionals and users.

## 7.1. TESTING

It is very important for a software project aimed at direct user service to constantly test the results and consistently monitor its working. Testing of software design has been discussed in the last chapter. The current chapter presents a brief discussion about the testing done to verify the correctness of results retrieved by the system with an illustrative example of output.

### 7.1.1. User in the Driver's Seat

Content personalization has been pursued right from the beginning as a useful extension of the Electronic SDI Service offered by the Central Library, utilizing the latest tools and techniques offered by database and web technology. Thus avoiding the issues which went wrong with Electronic SDI was of immediate concern for example, avoiding sending outputs by email since it flooded users' mailboxes besides creating excessive traffic in the LAN. Hence it was decided to make the information intermediary a mere facilitator and put the user in the driver's seat by letting him decide what service to select, which terms to include, how frequently to conduct the search, what format and order to use in displaying the results retrieved etc. This approach, however, leaves the system developers with limited knowledge and provides merely implicit means regarding the system-user interaction, thus making it somewhat difficult to test the system.

### 7.1.2. Matching Terms in Retrieved Results with Terms in Users' Own Publications

The study found good matches in the testing using keywords, both from personalized search results and publications of the concerned faculty. Details of the testing carried out for one faculty member's output are illustrated below. The publications list of one researcher is taken for the purpose of testing the search terms. The following table (Table 7.1) shows the frequency of occurrence of keywords from his publications with search results from IEEE for the search term "spread spectrum and error control coding". This is not a perfect match since all the specializations are not searched and included. Further, these trial results have been obtained without interacting with the faculty concerned and hence many of the intricacies of the specialization are not represented and term relationships not considered at this stage. However, there is still a satisfactory matching of keywords and frequencies from the two sets of publications, indicating a correlation and the utility of SAI in fulfilling the purpose for which it was conceived.

*Table 7.1: Keyword Matching of Publications and SAI Search Results*

| ***Keywords*** | ***Frequency in own Publications*** | ***Frequency in Personalized Search Results from IEL*** |
|---|---|---|
| Frequency-hopped | 4 | 4 |
| Radio networks | 5 | |
| Spread spectrum | 5 | 14 |
| Fading | 4 | 5 |
| Error control coding | 5 | 2 |
| Asymptotic analysis | 1 | |
| Linear modulation | 2 | |
| Communication | 59 | 78 |
| Partial-band noise | 2 | |
| Ratio-threshold test | 1 | |
| Wireless Communications | 3 | |
| Networks | 8 | |
| Receiver | 6 | 5 |
| CDMA | 3 | |
| Optical | 1 | 4 |
| Fiber | | 13 |
| Sequential decoder | | 28 |
| FANO's algorithm | | 8 |
| Multiple Access | | 4 |

## 7.2. FEEDBACK

A schematic representation of the electronic SDI system is presented below to highlight the major differences in feedback collection with that of the content personalization system.

In the SDI Service, the feedback (see figure 7.1) received from faculty members includes the following information:

* Adding or deleting subject terms
* Appreciating the utility of service such as 'good', 'useful', 'interested in receiving further outputs', illustrative examples highlighting the receipt of useful references, general comments such as 'helpful in obtaining current information' etc.
* Critical comments and suggestions regarding the improvement of the service such as inclusion of additional databases to improve the journal coverage, linking with ILL/DDS services to provide full text of results selected by users etc.

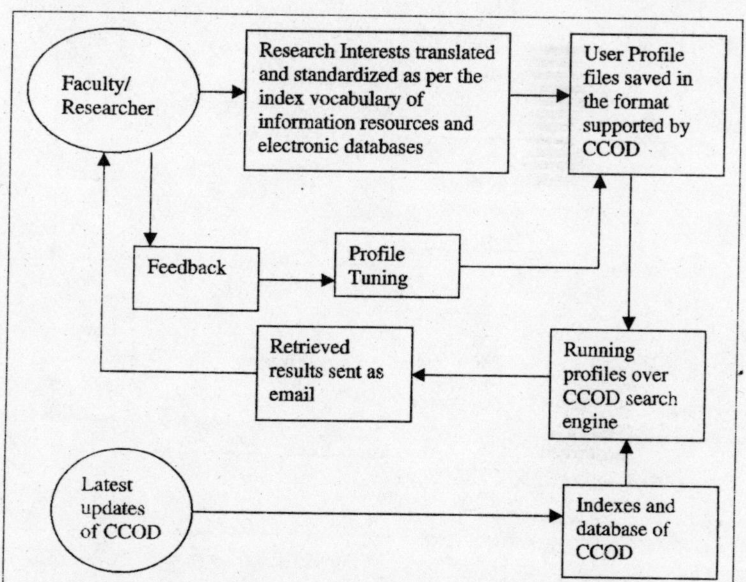


**Fig. 7.1: Schematic Representation of the Electronic SDI System**

Feedback received from the Personalization Service (see figure 7.2) focuses upon the following aspects:

* Suggestions for profile modification
* Appreciative comments about the service
* Critical comments regarding the extension of the content and style of service, apprehending the utility of such a service when e-journal and publisher portals already help to identify useful references
* Users' interest to have a single interface for search and retrieval of useful references from all resources subscribed by and accessed in the library
* Users being critical about the utility of some of the references provided by the system

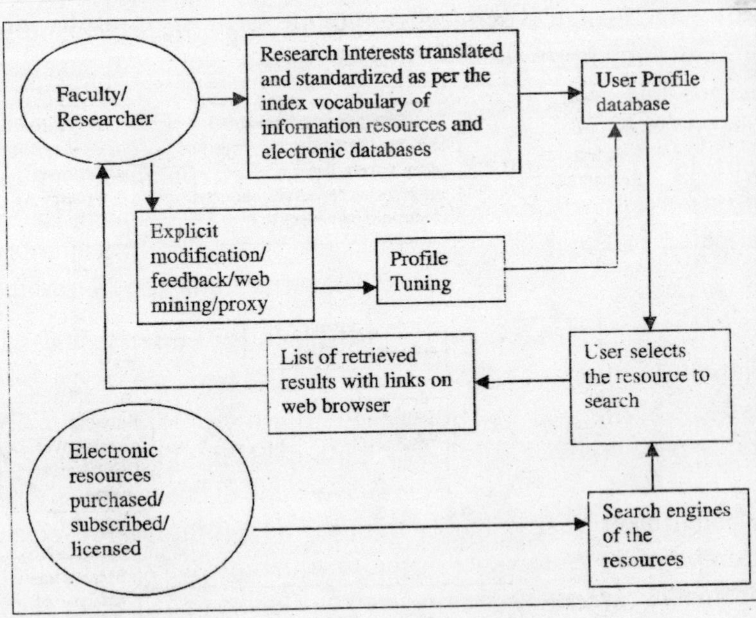


**Fig. 7.2: Schematic Representation of the Library Personalization System**

The feedback form designed to elicit users' comments is presented in Annexure 3.

## 7.3. IMPROVEMENTS

Some of the improvements currently under implementation or in the planning stage include:

* Identifying the increasing number of free web resources and merging them in a classified order with the existing resources
* Using different options for retrieving personalized search results (through the personalized page of individual faculty, by click and access mode from a hierarchical term listing etc.)
* Using standardized subject terms available in the discipline concerned to enhance the retrieval efficiency of users' terms
* Using clustering techniques for mapping the relation between terms, thus aiding context based retrieval
* Properly marking newly retrieved results by different search engines so that users need not refer to old results while scanning new ones
* Carrying on testing with searching in the background to do away with users accessing their pages and clicking on resources/typing for terms to be searched

## 7.4. MAINTENANCE

The server and PC will be maintained by the suppliers. Any difficulties in IP enabled access of e-journals would be addressed by publishers and their intermediaries. Problems in access as a result of technical faults at the campus level must be addressed by the network services of the Institute's Computer & Informatics Centre. Similarly, such faults in the library network would be taken care of by the System Analyst and support staff in the Computer Services Section. Any errors in the working of the SAI system will be corrected by the software developers working in the project. So far, after 18 months of operation, the system has not given any major technical or administrative problems.

The following chapter discusses further aspects like applications of personalization in other fields, problems and prospects, scope for further study and suggestions.

# Chapter 8
# Findings And Suggestions

## 8.0. INTRODUCTION

The previous chapter highlighted the details of testing of the working of the system and noted that no library personalization system works perfectly well because:

* User satisfaction differs from one person to another
* User conceptualization differs from one person to another
* User visualization of a particular term differs from one person to another

Thus the efforts made in collecting feedback from the target user group for attuning the system developed to the ever-changing interests of users have become crucial. The feedback collection and its functional incorporation into the system help to improve the utility of the personalization system. Maintenance steps ensure the constant working of the system to successfully handle the various tasks visualized even in the case of nonworking of any hardware or software tools. Based on the discussion in earlier chapters regarding the implemented model, this chapter attempts to conclude the study by exploring the steps involved in extension of the study to the other IITs, its viable and possible application in other fields, scope for further research as well as findings and suggestions.

## 8.1. UTILITY OF RESEARCH AND APPLICATIONS IN OTHER FIELDS

The current study has attempted to select the faculty users seeking information in same subject(s) of study or studies, preferably in narrow or specialized subject areas of study, in different branches of science, engineering, and technology. It has further tried to identify the essential concepts of subject interests of the sample users. The selected concepts form the basic criteria for defining the search terms and their relation to the different terms collected from a standard subject map. It has elicited correspondence between the sample literature, user information needs and search terms (concepts) for organizing and retrieving relevant information. Since the users' information needs and/or subject areas are in constant flux, the system attempts to develop general models for organizing literature and identifying the new concepts (terms) emerging in various study subjects and connecting them with the existing subject schema.

This study thus presents a novel approach to providing the required information support to researchers. Such proactive ways of selective information support will go a long way towards realizing/fulfilling the fundamental laws of library science. Libraries are increasingly facing grave challenges in the post-web information environment with more and more users looking outside the library for fulfillment of their information requirements, especially since traditional library practices are slow to devise new ways of selectively delivering the required information to users. Since the study is concerned with the collection and usage of resources procured in the library, the results of the study could also be extended to effective cost-benefit analysis of money spent and efforts undertaken for collection development. This would help in substantially improving the collection development exercises in the current scenario of libraries facing a serious financial crunch with the depreciation of the Indian currency on one hand and the increasing number of high quality resources warranting tough selection policies on the other. The effective management and personalization of digital contents will initiate and enhance similar practices in other libraries in the country, thus bridging the divide in information services in India and other industrially advanced countries. As contents can include anything from formal library sources to websites or customer information, the study could also be applied in commercial fields for identifying potential clients and in personalized delivery of products and information to them. Further, with more and more information resources getting populated on the web, this study could also be extended and applied to the vital issue of personalizing websites.

## 8.2. SCOPE FOR FURTHER RESEARCH

### 8.2.1. Hierarchical Classification

The present implementation focuses on identifying the faculty subject specialization from the terms suggested by him/her directly and alternatively, identifying the same from other relevant sources like research reports, institute publications, web sites, key words from publications, terms collected from proxy data etc. We have proposed a further research activity involving the need for arriving at a hierarchical classification for different subjects, and provision for searching based on this hierarchical structure. There are certain advantages with this type of implementation, especially since many faculty members cross specialize and hence can easily click on and access their areas of interest from the hierarchical subject map developed.

### 8.2.2. Identifying New References

Since many resources do not permit local archiving and bypassing of native search engines, the SAI personalization engine is designed to only collect the terms and post these to the native search engines. Hence by the very nature of their implementation, all matching records would be displayed. This may cause inconvenience to a frequent user, compelling him/her to continuously browse new as well as old resources. To counteract this problem, improvements in the search strategy specifically identifying the time of the last search and including this as a limiting factor in the search or identifying the record numbers of results from the last search and masking the same from new search (unless explicitly stated to do otherwise) are currently under testing.

### 8.2.3. Automatic Background Search

Currently the user needs to login to the SAI page and select the terms and resources to retrieve the matching results, which may involve considerable time (subject to network speed and use). An alternative to get over this limitation, currently under testing, is to search all the available resources using the suggested search terms at periodic intervals and keep it on the personalized web page or send it to the user as email, with links to the relevant full text resources.

### 8.2.4. Clustering and Reordering

The data obtained from the proxy server includes lot of unwanted information. Web usage mining techniques are therefore applied to extract the necessary information related to users' interests. Image files with extensions *gif, bmp* etc. are removed in data preprocessing stage, with subsequently cleaned data stored in the database. Users are identified by their individual IP- addresses and login ids. The URLs accessed by each user are retrieved from the database and the documents opened to extract each term present in the document. Stop words like 'a', 'an', 'the', 'from', 'to', 'for', 'and', 'then', 'thus' etc. are removed and the remaining terms stored in the database. For each term, the Term Frequency (TF), or the normalized frequency of the term in the document and the Inverse Document Frequency (IDF), the inverse of the proportion of documents in which the term appears, are calculated. Finally, the term weight is obtained as a product of TF and IDF. Terms whose term weight is greater than a specified threshold value are only considered for clustering and the remaining terms are deleted from the database. Search results can be reordered after clustering the documents for each user, requiring additional in-depth domain knowledge of the subject and the user concerned. The SAI system is designed to detect when a user runs a search, intercepts the results and finally checks each one against the closest cluster, based on recent history. This re-ranking is based on the TF-cosine similarity of each result page with the users' areas of interest - the most similar pages getting placed near the top of the list. Reordering of search results is achieved using the clustering technique which compares the clusters created based on recent history and displays the closest match on the top of the order list. Improving the clustering algorithms would thus help to achieve more accurate personalized search results. Incorporating the recommendation process in SAI is another possible upgradation of the library personalization system, designed as it is to support the information needs of faculty members and facilitate them in effectively conducting their teaching and research work. This application attempts to add value to the results returned by normal search engines by re-ranking them in such a way that the users' contexts are reflected, so that different users still get the same set of results, but ordered in such a way that the results more relevant to a particular user are ranked higher. Note that these are not quite personalized search results but can be taken just as a personalized ranking of the standard results.

### 8.2.5. Usage Studies of SAI

There is considerable difficulty in determining accurate and relevant user interests and mapping them effectively into the products and services offered by the library. Also, user interests are characterized by continuous change. In the event of multiple users sharing the same PC, it is difficult to identify each individual user in the absence of one to one mapping between users and IP addresses. Continuously changing IP addresses also pose a problem. The success and continuation of personalization and related proactive client-centric information service needs an integrated and functional user interest management system for the library. However, it is difficult to implement the same in the near future for many libraries due to their increasing dependence on publisher and aggregator centric solutions which focus less on standardization and more on commercial interests. Another crucial area for future study includes steps to evaluate the usefulness of the SAI system by identifying the data retrieved by it and accessed by the users, as evident from proxy logs, general feedback about the service, term modifications, ease of use etc.

### 8.2.6. Extension of SAI to the Other IITs

The other IITs can configure individual systems on the lines of SAI by creating profiles of their faculty members and conducting the personalization service accordingly. Another alternative involves uploading faculty profiles to the SAI server, creating hyperlinks on their local servers and informing faculty members about the availability of the service. Following extension of the service utilizing any of these options, the utility of the system needs to be evaluated to assess the information access features available to faculty members in different institutions.

## 8.3. MAJOR FINDINGS

This study attempted to explore the extension of personalization techniques in the Indian context to electronic full text content of interest to research and teaching in premier technical libraries of the IITs by basing IIT Kharagpur as a model. Pragmatic applications of the nascent web technology tools and age-old user profiling techniques of library and information science stand to benefit users immensely. This will undoubtedly lead to better usage of information resources by optimizing the time available with users to target increasingly specialized resources, as envisioned by the fundamental laws of library science. Further improvements in the personalization system developed will be apparent with usage of the existing implementation, usage driven feedback and feedback based modifications.

### 8.3.1. Proactive Information Services

Libraries have traditionally concentrated more on collection development and information organization, with services and their qualitative improvement normally occupying the least priority. Consortia based access to e-resources has provided libraries with the strength and expertise to vouch for collection development and information organization, and also for improving information services rendered at a particular member site. Each of the IIT libraries should strive for optimal usage of INDEST resources to provide effective and efficient information support for ongoing teaching and research activities. Instead of merely facilitating access to INDEST resources by alerting the user community about resources available, evolving a proactive service for personalizing consortia contents will definitely improve the library's image and augment the confidence of its clientele on a hitherto predominantly passive service organization.

### 8.3.2. Effective Use Measurement and Evaluation of Resources

Usage quantification is the best way to evaluate the utility of information resources procured in a library. With printed sources, there is always some difficulty in assessing the actual use, as most of the manual records and usage statistics from library automation systems fail to provide micro level usage reports. The personalization server would be able to deliver both qualitative and quantitative usage parameters, indirectly acting as a vital evaluation tool for assessing the utility of INDEST resources. User feedback on new resources along with usage reports of existing ones would further help to arrive at new resources and delete less used existing ones if required.

### 8.3.3. Creation of Expert Database

The user profiles with exhaustive details of subject specialization of in-house researchers would also act as an expert database, helping to identify potential experts for consultancy work and sponsored research.

### 8.3.4. Saving of Researchers' Time

Though users have been provided with additional resources through consortia, they may find it difficult to search and access many of these resources in limited time at their disposal to conduct highly competitive technology research. It is imperative that information professionals trained in identifying, tracking, organizing, searching and selecting relevant sources through the personalization system should save and conserve the time of researchers, which can thus be better utilized for serious research activity.

### 8.3.5. Boosting the Image of Journal/Computer Sections

Unlike the book-related sections in a library which enjoy the benefit of better bibliographic control, journal sections are often faced with problems related to the peculiarities of publishing and distributing journals. Since journals are subscribed to and paid for in advance, the focal activity of the section revolves around continuously monitoring the supply of all issues, which not many libraries are lucky enough to get. Due to missing issues, further processing of these volumes often gets delayed. Further, there are multiple problems related to maintaining loose and bound journals. Nowadays, online access to subscribed journals has helped the journal section in getting better visibility. Content personalization would further enhance journal usage besides the library's image as a whole and the journal related sections in particular. Same is the case with the computer sections in the library which, instead of acting as mute facilitators for accessing the existing resources, can aggressively go about providing user centered services through personalizing electronic contents. Library personalization would also be taken as more pragmatic means for e-journal and e-content management.

## 8.4. PROBLEMS AND PROSPECTS

Some of the problems identified and their possible solutions for stabilizing the personalized information system in the libraries of IITs are:

### 8.4.1. Multiple Systems

IIT Libraries being equipped with many of the contents and solutions essential for a personalization system in a multitude of systems, what is required is to focus on a single system to deal with all the library operations and services. Since most of these libraries use commercial library automation systems, customization is required to provide an open source interface to access these proprietary solutions or a library personalization system's interface to access the backend of the library database system. Similarly, web and consortia access of journals always constrained the libraries to do them only through publishers' website links. When cumulation and management of these journals is required, the solution offered involves a j-gate/ingenta sort of approach, redirecting to links in distributed servers. However, this is not considered to be a very intelligent approach. What is required especially for IIT libraries is to create and develop a proprietary system that may appear like a single system aggregating the individual systems to work in the background with the personalized system to search and access the different e-journals so that users do not have to bother about the formalities of the solution providers and the access passwords/IPs.

### 8.4.2. Need for Client Side Personalization

Both faculty members and researchers in the IITs being heavily loaded with teaching and academic work, getting them to invest time for tuning their profiles and specializations becomes a difficult proposition. Thus, libraries must utilize indirect methods of monitoring user interests such as usage monitoring at the individual user/PC (client access) level for INDEST resources and other electronic services offered. Cassel and Wolz have suggested client side architecture where the search tool resides on the user's system, consequently the user's preferences and search history can be recorded and consulted as and when needed. An integrated user interest management system will help libraries to optimize their finances on more useful purchases, specialized delivery of existing services and starting of new services. There are further difficulties in getting usage parameters from the Institute Proxy servers besides the existing technical limitations of collecting all required parameters from the local

SAI proxy, since some of the required information gets screened at the Institute proxy itself.

### 8.4.3. Personnel Problems

There is doubt not only on the part of users but also the library professionals regarding the utility and benefit of personalization, customization, personal links, quick searches etc. Users have their reservations about library professionals' ability to understand and map their complex specializations into personalization systems, whereas professionals are busy engaged in their routine professional tasks and essential IT applications of database creation and support, leaving very little time to think, plan and execute fresh services.

### 8.4.4. Standards

In the absence of very few projects and solutions, there is the issue of lack of standards in describing resources and user profiling as well as the modalities of setting up the personalization system and operating the services. Also, for personalization systems to mature, a strong base of electronic resources is required which is unfortunately lacking in many of our libraries. Though IIT libraries are equipped with a good set of external resources, the internal digital library component is still not very substantial and for this, libraries have to concentrate on various fronts like digitizing locally owned resources, hosting institute generated academic and research information etc. along with creating a single window information facility for external resources to replace the existing multiple systems.

### 8.4.5. Managing User Interests

#### *8.4.5.1. Quantifying Use*

It is difficult as such to quantify use since the library statistics deal only with explicit use; however, there also exists implicit use (browsing, consulting etc.), which is too arduous to be quantified. Simultaneously, there are vital questions about whether merely issuing a book or taking a photocopy of a journal article constitutes use, and this warrants qualitative assessment of use. How many libraries have assessed journal use by quantifying the use of individual articles from loose issues? Even the usage statistics for full text journal access through consortia fail to provide the qualitative aspects of use. Merely clicking a link, downloading a page or holding a page in the desktop while availing a coffee break may not attribute to use in real terms.

### *8.4.5.2. Representing User Preferences*

The central issue is how effectively and intelligently the personalization setup can capture and represent the user preferences based on the books issued, books requested, articles referred or cited etc. The personalization mechanism and the user interest gathering tools it utilizes should be able to utilize input from users as well as capture information based on self-learning from observable use patterns. In many cases, the feedback mechanism fails to work as interactively as desired because of the library professionals' focus on 'recall' compared to users' preference for 'precision'. Artificial Intelligence techniques need to be explored for dynamic profile modification and optimization using filtering agents, intelligent agents etc. in the light of estimated use behavior. Several use and user centered attributes reside in the client machines; hence the success of personalization tasks depends to a large extent on collecting this data. This is essential to learn about and represent user interests, the contents actually used etc., all of which involve further developmental challenges.

### *8.4.5.3. Poor User Professional Interaction*

In many cases, users are forced to scan lengthy SDI and CAS printouts due to the inherent difficulties relating to concrete expression of information requirements and the problems of information processing and retrieval. The library professionals, while matching suggested search terms and their relationships, sometimes discard some relevant information on the one hand and add some noise on the other. The users also lack the patience to constantly interact with the library staff for refining their profiles and improving the relevance of information services, mainly due to time constraints and/or doubts regarding the efficacy of the service provided. Going by a rough assessment, it is doubtful whether more than 10% of the users respond to the SDI results provided, the majority either using them as they are or rejecting them straightaway. Out of those who respond, only a few show any willingness to provide constant feedback for modifying their information requirements or keywords, for the purpose of improving the utility of such services.

#### *8.4.5.4. User Interest Management System*

The user interests identified are to be incorporated into a suitable database engine for providing access to users in a restrictive fashion so that users can modify their profiles as and when needed without professional intervention. However, care should be taken not to disclose others profiles to a user, so that s/he can browse only some schematic patterns of group interests. Profiles are further to be constructed at both individual and group levels to render different types of services. This may necessitate various iterations and refinements based on feedback and search output relating to interest profiles. Since information retrieval is based on the search terms selected, for profile based matching, it is necessary to identify the essential concepts of the subject specialization of the users, including correspondence with the key words used to index resources. While mechanisms to generate information continue to grow in number and sophistication, tools and techniques to manage, filter, and search information lag behind [**Bonett**]. An efficient user interest management system will interface with one or more content servers in a distributed environment to extract contents of interest and concern to individual users.

#### *8.4.5.5. Attracting Users*

Many a time, the library needs to attract users to provide suitable feedback regarding its services and overall organization.

However, encouraging comments and suitable responses may not be forthcoming initially. For example, when the Central Library of IIT Kharagpur introduced the Electronic SDI service in May 1997 [**Jeevan**] to alert and update the researchers at regular intervals about new developments in their chosen fields of specialization, sample profiles were constructed from the subject interests of faculty listed in the 'Annual Report' of the institute, which were later updated based on the feedback received from the individuals concerned. It is always good to offer something new to the users before seeking something from them, since in this way they will be more attracted towards and involved in the library's initiatives.

### 8.4.6. Difficulties in Personalizing INDEST Contents

#### *8.4.6.1. No local hosting*

All electronic resources being subscribed through INDEST shall be available from the publishers' websites, local hosting of resources not having been considered at this stage [**Arora and Agrawal**]. ICOLC demands that consortia and their member libraries should be allowed to take all reasonable steps to archive content purchased or leased by them [**Hirshon** *et al.*]. Publishers should accept responsibility for archiving and providing continuing access to their published content and should not discourage individual libraries, consortia, national libraries or other third parties from developing alternative solutions for archiving electronic journal content. When an information provider provides access to data from its website (rather than through local mounting of data), the provider should guarantee perpetual availability of the content [**Hirshon** *et al.*]. Consortia or libraries that wish to mount information locally should be permitted to do so on the system of their choice and licenses should not limit the right of a library or a consortium to integrate the data into local system infrastructures and information services [**Hirshon** *et al.*]. Though local hosting and archiving of contents is discussed and agreed upon with some publishers/vendors, the modus operandi of the INDEST content access in the IITs so far is through publishers' websites [**Arora and Agrawal**].

Future plans of INDEST Consortium would include setting-up mirror servers, local hosting etc. [**Arora and Agrawal**]. The problem regarding local hosting needs to be addressed with respect to the clauses in the license agreement, especially those relating to the nature and type of access rights and the number of simultaneous accesses. It has also been proposed that the Licensors should be permitted to download bibliographic records and abstracts in their local database (especially records for publications from their own faculty, staff and students) and full-text articles of their faculty and staff to their Institute's e-print archives [**Arora and Agrawal**]. Regarding archival backup, the INDEST license agreement has asked the publishers to provide perpetual access to the subscribed resources even after termination of subscription for the period for which the subscription was paid, along with the backup on CD / DVD or any other electronic media in a suitable format [**Arora and Agrawal**].

#### *8.4.6.2. Not many resources provide personalization*

Out of all INDEST contents, only 'web of science' has so far indicated its interest to incorporate personalization features into the product, enabling users to save search strategies on their desktop or on the ISI Web of Knowledge server [**ISI**]. An alert management page will allow users to quickly change search and alert options, and a personal journal list feature will offer seamless integration between ISI Web of Knowledge and the most recent journal table of contents information in ISI Current Contents Connect [**ISI**]. In the absence of such proprietary solutions, the library will need to fine-tune its personalization system to work with multiple search engines and software.

#### *8.4.6.3. Increased access base and behavioural aspects of use*

The INDEST consortium has enabled all its beneficiaries to increase the number of accessible full text resources from a few hundred to over four thousand [**Arora and Agrawal**]. This, combined with electronic access to journals which have not been subscribed as part of the consortium has lead to a greatly widened access base in the IITs, which may further lead to certain behavioural aspects of information use. It may take a little more time for the old users to get familiarized with many of the new resources and new users with all the resources. Then only better assessment of usage of these resources can be done.

#### *8.4.6.4. Relevance Assessment*

Having the advantage of subject knowledge, a researcher conducting an information search may normally not follow a linear approach, instead proceeding with new areas or qualifiers to the search process to arrive at a few relevant results. S/he may also abandon or abort a search immediately after assessing the utility of results. However, an information professional, being a master of the searching process only, is obviously handicapped at relevance assessment level and may arrive at a list where many results are not totally relevant to the user. We follow pattern matching and frequency of occurrence of certain patterns to retrieve relevant resources and it may so happen that two documents dealing with entirely different contexts of a particular topic or altogether diverse topics may have the same patterns and frequency distribution. Searches conducted by information professionals would typically also look for complete recall rather than total relevance, leading to a large number of low relevance results, further undermining the confidence of the user. Hence, professionals need to refine information mining skills with the aid of special thesaurus systems and even by using expert systems on the subject to overcome the limitations of search engines.

### 8.4.7. Subject Terms

The biggest challenge in the development of the SAI personalization system is to attract and sustain user interest since researchers are generally too engrossed in their teaching and research activities to spare time for interaction with library personnel. Such interaction is vital in understanding and representing their subject specialization in profiles for effective personalization. The existing information infrastructure in the IITs conforms to high standards; further, with the rapid spread and increasing acceptance of electronic resources, users are virtually bypassing libraries to fulfill many of their information requirements, preferring to bank upon the expertise of their friends and peers rather than the library staff for assistance. Thus the need of the hour is to improve the library's service-providing and user-friendly aspect so that any hesitation on the users' part in approaching the library staff to address their information requirements is minimized, thereby helping to improve existing services as well as implementing new ones. Users need to realize that the time and effort they invest in creating a better and lively representation of their subject interests will benefit them in the long run in the form of frequent relevant outputs from the system. In the context of a higher academic center like the IIT, researchers' subject interests continuously change and the system therefore needs to be alert enough to gather and map these so as to be more attractive and current to users.

Assigning standardized subject terms to the personalization system for greater precision and relevance in retrieval calls for a special keyword assignment system. This requires considerable effort in compiling the subject terms and subsequently grouping them as broader and narrower, with synonyms requiring the support of a subject expert. However, successfully completing the task for a few departments provided us with a fresh insight to undertake it for other departments too. Since the system developed consists of an exhaustive list of subjects of interest to the Institute's faculty and research community, it could be effectively utilized for making intelligent decisions regarding other services like addition of new books, subscription to new journals etc. It could additionally be used to provide vital inputs about implementing future programmes and services. The system would also help in identifying experts for supervising impending research and consultancy projects.

Subject heading lists and thesauri are unavailable for certain disciplines whereas multiple sources describing different classification are available for certain others. Thus, identification and selection of subject terms often becomes complex, particularly due to their dynamic nature in reflecting the present research activity in the discipline concerned as well as aiding and assisting suitable retrievals in current areas. Intelligence and self-learning being integral components of a personalization system, a subject term classification and retrieval system to learn and represent new terms based on a well described heuristics and knowledge representation system needs to be developed.

## 8.5. SUGGESTIONS

To help other libraries interested in venturing into such client centered information services, an attempt has been made here to highlight the essential steps involved in developing personalized information services:

### 8.5.0. Subscribing to Electronic Resources

Subscribing to the right set of electronic resources of maximum interest to users is a primary requirement in the operation of personalized information services. Resources are in plenty and often costly, necessitating the need for proper selection and evaluation of the subscribed resources. The ideal framework is to collect the requirements from individual researchers, sections or departments and then to arrive at a shortlist satisfying each and every major constituent of the Institution. This shortlist may require detailed evaluation by an expert committee to study the features of each resource and evaluate how best it meets both individual and collective requirements. Budget also acts as major deciding criteria due to the costs involved and fixed budget allocations. Resources once identified and subscribed are to be constantly assessed on the basis of whether they meet the continuously changing research and academic requirements of the Institution. If any of them fails to meet the target, they are to be eliminated and fresh resources are to be added. All resources which meet the evaluation criteria are also to be renewed to ensure the successful operation of personalization system for a longer duration.

### 8.5.1. Procuring Hardware/Software

Since usage and expectations of the system undergo drastic improvements, it is always ideal to arrive at a modular structure for procuring hardware so that upgradations on the existing system could be made later without altogether dismantling the existing one. Instead of opting for proprietary solutions, it is best to work with open source systems (such as mySQL as database engine and Linux as operating system) and web based programming tools like php and javascripts for the programming aspects. Though tailor made solutions are available and possible for personalization work, the library can stick to freely available simple tools to achieve the desired matching of resources as per the specialized interests of its clientele. However, preference should always be given to current tools and techniques so that the system developed may work without errors for a decent span of time.

### 8.5.2. Electronic Literacy of Users

Users must be well acquainted with electronic gadgets to derive maximum benefits of electronic information products. The INDEST Consortium has very rightly accorded maximum importance to the training of information professionals and information users, with libraries attached to the IITs naturally taking advantages of such training. The Digital Library attached to the Central Library of IIT Kharagpur conducts two training programmes of 1 hour duration every week to brief new users about the electronic information resources available in the library and how users can use them to the best of their educational and research purpose. Only users with high electronic information literacy can put the subscribed resources to optimum use, justifying the purpose of resources channeled to acquire these costly resources.

### 8.5.3. Continuing Education of Information Professionals

Library professionals should be exposed to the latest in information technology for implementing technology based information solutions in individual libraries. A library can reap the maximum potential of electronic information only if its staff members maintain a positive attitude towards technology. The management should further take special care to ensure that the new products and technology procured are easily accessible to all interested staff members so as to prevent undue exposure to technology by a particular category of staff or an individual. Apart from encouraging library professionals to take up specialized courses in computer applications and information technology, the library management should also liberally sponsor them to attend workshops, tutorials, conferences etc. They may also be given paid membership subscriptions to professional societies, professional associations and professional journals. These steps would help staff members appreciate the special importance the management attaches to their professional growth, making them more responsible, representative and participative in electronic enabling of library organization and information services.

### 8.5.4. Budget

Sufficient budgetary provision must be made not only to procure electronic information resources and the necessary hardware and software but also to fulfill the training requirements of both users and staff. Many libraries operate on the premise that subscription and licensing of electronic resources hold the key. However, this is just an initial step and it must be clearly underlined that only when the professional staff members possess some expertise and experience in the resources subscribed, can they successfully disseminate the same to library users busy in their assigned vocations.

### 8.5.5. Institutional Support

Institutional support is important and greatly required for the library to plan and execute such services. The mindset of the organization and its people, especially the top management, can play a crucial role in supporting the Library to achieve the required infrastructure, necessary technical support and sufficient monetary aid to successfully implement the different strategies and achieve the major objectives as far as electronic information and personalized information services are concerned. A modern library should be conducted more as an academic unit rather than as an administrative section.

## 8.6. CONCLUSION

Rather than merely facilitating access to electronic resources by alerting the user community about the available resources, evolution of a proactive service for electronic content personalization will definitely improve the library's image besides further augmenting the confidence of its clientele. In the current scenario, libraries can discard their image of predominantly passive service organizations only by bringing fresh insight into old services and venturing into new ones with age-old expertise in information consolidation and repackaging. Any personalization service or other user focused and client response driven service relating to electronic information must at some point or the other make constructive efforts towards identifying and mapping user interests, merging these interest profiles in an integrated fashion so as to interface with all aspects of library work like collection development and information services, leading to the betterment of each of these activities. Managing users' dynamic subject interests and information requirements involves sprucing up the existing library and information management activities. It is highly required for all concerned to rethink, adapt their time tested skills and interface them with the latest customer care tools and techniques to further improve library services and give users their rightful place in library and information activities. The IIT Kharagpur model of personalizing electronic information, SAI, will undoubtedly motivate many other libraries in the country to devise similar solutions so that library resources are put to optimum use by connecting relevant information with targeted potential users.

## REFERENCES

1. **Arora** (Jagdish) and **Agrawal** (Pawan). Indian Digital Library in Engineering Science and Technology (INDEST) Consortium: Consortia-Based Subscription to Electronic Resources for Technical Education System in India: A Government of India Initiative. International CALIBER 2003, Ahmedabad, 13-15 February 2003. In Proceedings Volume - Mapping Technology on Libraries and People. 2003. INFLIBNET Centre. Ahmedabad. p 271-290.

2. **Bonett** (Monica). Personalization of Web Services: Opportunities and Challenges, *Ariadne*. 28. http:// www.ariadne.ac.uk /issue28/personalization/intro.html

3. **Cassel** (Lillian) and **Wolz** (Ursula). Client Side Personalization.

4. http://www.ercim.org/publication/ws-proceedings/ DelNoe02/CasselWolz.pdf

5. **Hirshon** (Arnold) et al. Statement of Current Perspective and Preferred Practices for the Selection and Purchase of Electronic Information. International Coalition of Library Consortia (ICOLC). http://www.library.yale.edu/consortia/ statement.html

6. **ICOLC, 1.** International Coalition of Library Consortia (ICOLC). Guidelines for Statistical Measures of Usage of Web-Based Information Resources (December 2001 revision of November 1998 Guidelines). http:// www.library.yale.edu/consortia/ 2001webstats.htm

7. **ICOLC, 2.** International Coalition of Library Consortia (ICOLC). Statement of Current Perspective and Preferred Practices for the Selection and Purchase of Electronic Information. Update No. 1: New Developments In E-Journal Licensing (December 2001 update to March 1998 Statement). http://www.library.yale.edu/consortia/ 2001currentpractices.htm

8. **ISI.** Personalization and Alerting to be added to ISI Web of Knowledge. http://www.isinet.com/isi/news/2002news/isi/8146251/

9. **Jeevan** (V K J). Developing an Electronic SDI service at the Indian Institute of Technology, Kharagpur. Program. 33, 2; Apr 1999; p 157-161.

# Annexure 1

# Content Personalization in IIT LIBRARIES

## (Questionnaire for Librarian/ Acting Librarian)

**Note:**

1. Please be brief and objective in your response. Kindly tick only suitable options where multiple options are provided.
2. Separate sheets may be used if the space provided is insufficient.
3. Please don't forget to attach the Institute's Annual Report for the last three years as well as user library guides

**1. LIBRARY PROFILE**

Name of the Library:

Year of establishment:

Mailing Address:

Telephone:

Fax:

Email Address:

Website URL (If available):

**2. COLLECTION**

Please indicate the total number of volumes (as on........):

Books:

Current Periodicals: Indian: Foreign:

Bound Volumes of periodicals:

Standards: Patents: Theses:

Audio cassettes: Video cassettes: Microforms:

Others (Please specify):

**3. ELECTRONIC INFORMATION**

Please specify the availability of electronic information (Indicate total number as on ):

Electronic Journals in CD:

Through web access:

E-books:

Web:

CD-ROMs:

Floppies:

Any other format (please specify):

Electronic Databases Media:

CD-ROMs:

Floppies:

Web:

Any other (please specify):

Electronic Databases Type:

Bibliographic:

Full Text:

Any other (please specify):

(Please attach in a separate sheet, if possible, a list of databases, electronic journals and e-books with subject breakup).

**4. FORMAT PREFERENCE**

If a document is available in several formats, which format is given preference in your library?

Paper form

Electronic Form

Microform

Please indicate the reason for the same:

**5. E-JOURNALS**

Do you subscribe to journals in electronic format?

☐ Yes ☐ No

(a) If yes, please indicate the type of periodicals acquired:

Indexing and abstracting periodicals ☐

Full text periodicals (current) ☐

Back volumes of periodicals ☐

Please indicate the reason(s) for acquiring journals in electronic format:

Economic to acquire ☐

Solves the problem of theft and mutilation ☐

Easy to maintain ☐

Provides networking facility ☐

Solves the space problem ☐

Any other (please specify) ☐

(b) If you don't subscribe to electronic journals, state the reason(s) for the same:

Initial expenditure on infrastructure very high ☐

Staff unwilling to handle electronic formats ☐

Readers resist use of electronic format ☐

Required journals not available in electronic format ☐

Subscription too expensive ☐

Any other (please specify) ☐

**6. BUDGET**

Please indicate the budget for the last three years:

**a. 2000-2001:**

a) Institute Budget: Rs.

b) Library Budget: Rs.

(Please state budget for the following categories)

Books:

Current Periodicals:

Electronic Sources:

Equipment:

Hardware:

Software:

Others (please specify):

**b. 1999-2000:**

a) Institute Budget: Rs.

b) Library Budget: Rs.

(Please state budget for the following categories)

Books:

Current Periodicals:

Electronic Sources:

Equipment:

Hardware:

Software:

Others (please specify):

**c. 1998-1999:**

a) Institute Budget: Rs.

b) Library Budget: Rs.

(Please state budget for the following categories)

Books:

Current Periodicals:

Electronic Sources:

Equipment:

Hardware:

Software:

Others (please specify):

d. Is the above allocation (for different heads) fixed or revised from year to year?

Fixed ☐

Revised from year to year ☐

e. In your opinion the budget spent on IT-related products is:

More than appropriate ☐

Appropriate ☐

Less than appropriate ☐

7. **LIBRARY STAFF**

Strength of Library Staff (Indicate number)

Librarian:

Deputy Librarians:

Assistant Librarians:

System Analysts:

STAs:

TAs:

Clerical:

Attendants:

Support:

Mechanics:

Others (please specify):

8. **HARDWARE**

(Indicate number)

Unix Servers:

NT Servers:

NT Workstations:

Multimedia PCs:

PCs:

VT100/Dumb Terminals:

Any other (please specify):

(If a list of machines with their configurations is available, please attach a copy of the same)

**9. SOFTWARE**

(Please specify details under each head)

Operating System:

Library Automation Software Package:

Word Processing:

Database software:

Networking Software:

Multimedia:

Any other (please specify):

(If a list of software with their versions is prepared, is available, please attach a copy of the same)

**10. CURRENT AWARENESS SERVICES (CAS)**

Please indicate details about the Current Awareness Services (CAS) offered by your Library:

**a. Printed**

**Databases/Sources Used:**

Is the service:

Profile based ☐ Subject based ☐

General ☐

**User Category:**

Faculty ☐ Technical Staff ☐

Research Scholars ☐ PG ☐

UG ☐ All ☐

Is the service free or paid?

Free ☐ Paid ☐

Have you extended the service to outside users?

Yes ☐ No ☐

If yes, what are the modalities?

**Frequency:**

Weekly ☐ Fortnightly ☐

Monthly ☐ Bimonthly ☐

Quarterly ☐ Irregular ☐

Any other (please specify) ☐

**Output Format** (Specify any standard formats used. If not, indicate the type of information provided such as author, title, etc.):

**Usage:**

Heavily used ☐ Moderately used ☐

Less used ☐

**User Satisfaction:**

High ☐ Average ☐

Not Satisfied ☐

**b. Electronic**

**Databases/Sources Used:**

Is the service:

Profile based ☐ Subject based ☐

General ☐

**User Category:**

Faculty ☐ Technical Staff ☐

Research Scholars ☐ PG ☐

UG ☐ All ☐

Is the service free or paid?

Free ☐ Paid ☐

Have you extended the service to outside users?

Yes ☐ No ☐

If yes, what are the modalities?

**Frequency:**

Weekly ☐ Fortnightly ☐

Monthly ☐ Bimonthly ☐

Quarterly ☐ Irregular ☐

Any other (please specify)

Indicate the Software used and give a brief description of the same:

Is it developed In-house or a Commercial Package?

In-house ☐

Commercial Package ☐

**Output Format** (Specify any standard formats used. If not, indicate the type of information provided such as author, title etc.):

**Usage:**

Heavily used ☐ Moderately used ☐

Less used ☐

**User Satisfaction:**

High ☐ Average ☐

Not Satisfied ☐

## 11. SELECTIVE DISSEMINATION OF INFORMATION (SDI) SERVICE

Please indicate details about the Selective Dissemination of Information (SDI) Services offered by your Library:

**a. Printed**

**Databases/Sources Used:**

**Mechanism used to construct the User Profiles** (If standard forms are used to elicit user interest, please attach copies of the same):

**User Category:**

Faculty ☐ Technical Staff ☐

Research Scholars ☐ PG ☐

UG ☐ All ☐

Is the service free or paid?

Free ☐ Paid ☐

Have you extended the service to outside users?

Yes ☐ No ☐

If yes, what are the modalities?

**Frequency:**

Weekly ☐ Fortnightly ☐

Monthly ☐ Bimonthly ☐

Quarterly ☐ Irregular ☐

Any other (please specify)

**Output Format** (specify any standard formats used. If not, indicate the type of information provided such as author, title etc.):

**Usage:**

Heavily used ☐ Moderately used ☐

Less used ☐

**User Satisfaction:**

High ☐ Average ☐

Not Satisfied ☐

b. **Electronic**

**Databases/Sources Used:**

**Mechanism used to construct the User Profiles** (If standard forms are used to elicit user interest, please attach copies of the same):

Describe the steps taken to create and optimize profiles, and indicate how the feedback mechanism tunes the profiles:

User Category:

Faculty ☐ Technical Staff ☐

Research Scholars ☐ PG ☐

UG ☐ All ☐

Is the service free or paid?

Free ☐ Paid ☐

Have you extended the service to outside users?

Yes ☐ No ☐

If yes, what are the modalities?

**Frequency:**

Weekly ☐ Fortnightly ☐

Monthly ☐ Bimonthly ☐

Quarterly ☐ Irregular ☐

Any other (please specify)

Indicate the **Software** used and give a brief description of the same:

Is it developed In-house or a Commercial Package?

In-house ☐ Commercial Package ☐

**Output Format** (Specify any standard formats used. If not, indicate the type of information provided such as author, title etc.):

**Usage:**

Heavily used ☐ Moderately used ☐

Less used ☐

**User Satisfaction:**

High ☐ Average ☐

Not Satisfied ☐

**12. CD-ROM SEARCH SERVICES**

Are you offering CD-ROM search services?

Yes ☐ No ☐

If yes, indicate the **Databases Covered:**

**Frequency:**

Weekly ☐ Fortnightly ☐

Monthly ☐ Bimonthly ☐

Quarterly ☐ Irregular ☐

Any other (please specify)

**User Category:**

Faculty ☐ Technical Staff ☐

Research Scholars ☐ PG ☐

UG ☐ All ☐

Is the search conducted by:

Users ☐

Library Professionals ☐

Are you using Profiles for these services?

Yes ☐ No ☐

Is there any periodic delivery of fresh search results of new database updates to users?

Yes ☐ No ☐

If yes, indicate whether it's through:

email ☐ Print ☐

ftp ☐

Any other (please specify)

**13. FULL TEXT INFORMATION SERVICES**

Are any full text CAS/SDI Services are being offered?

Yes ☐ No ☐

If yes, indicate the **Databases/Sources** used:

Indicate whether it is:

Profile based ☐ Subject based ☐

General ☐

**User Category:**

Faculty ☐ Technical Staff ☐

Research Scholars ☐ PG ☐

UG ☐ All ☐

Is the service free or paid?

Free ☐ Paid ☐

Have you extended the service to outside users?

Yes ☐ No ☐

If yes, what are the modalities?

**Frequency:**

Weekly ☐ Fortnightly ☐

Monthly ☐ Bimonthly ☐

Quarterly ☐ Irregular ☐

Any other (please specify)

Indicate the **Software** used and give a brief description of the same:

Is it developed In-house or a Commercial Package?

In-house ☐

Commercial Package ☐

**Mechanism used to construct the User Profiles** (If standard forms are used to elicit user interest, please attach copies of the same):

If profile based, describe the steps taken to create and optimize profiles, and indicate how the feedback mechanism tunes the profiles:

**Output Format** (specify any standard formats used. If not, indicate the type of information provided such as author, title etc.):

**Usage:**

Heavily used ☐ Moderately used ☐

Less used ☐

**User Satisfaction:**

High ☐ Average ☐

Not Satisfied ☐

If full text services are not offered, list the constraints in devising such services in your library:

**14. USER PREFERENCES**

a. How do user preferences affect your library in the following areas?

Collection Development of Books/Journals/Other Sources ☐

Developing user services ☐

b. What is your opinion about User Interest Management?

c. Do you interact with users through Questionnaires/ Input through web forms etc., to elicit their views on library organization and services?

Yes ☐ No ☐

If yes, the details:

d. Are you considering user issue patterns for new acquisitions apart from written requests?

Yes ☐ No ☐

If yes, what is the percentage of preference assigned to each?

e. Are books taken out for study in Reading Halls marked for use?

Yes ☐ No ☐

f. Do statistics regarding photocopy services serve as a tangible measure of use assessed for future acquisitions of Books and Journals?

Yes ☐ No ☐

g. Do you interact with users through Questionnaires/ Input through web forms etc., for profile construction and modification?

Yes ☐ No ☐

If yes, the details:

h. Are you constructing user profiles to match user preferences?

Yes ☐ No ☐

If yes, for what types of services:

i. What is the mechanism used to construct user profiles? (Please attach copies of standard forms, if any used to elicit user interests)

j. If profiles are used, describe the steps taken to create and optimize profiles, and how the feedback mechanism from users tunes the profiles:

k. What are the different tools and techniques from Library and Information Science for profile construction, modification and tuning?

l. Do you consider use patterns like usage statistics and use behavior from library databases, records kept at ILL/ Resource Sharing unit, Reprography Section etc. also in the construction of user profiles?

Yes ☐ No ☐

m. If so, what are the mechanisms used to assess and quantify use patterns?

n. What is your opinion regarding incorporation of use behavior in profiles?

o. Are Artificial Intelligence (AI) techniques used for dynamic modification and optimization of profiles using filtering agents, intelligent agents etc. in the light of estimated use behavior?

Yes ☐ No ☐

**15. DATA MINING APPLICATIONS**

What are the data mining applications your Library is

involved in to enhance the utility of locally acquired / leased content?

**16. CONTENT PERSONALIZATION**

a) Are you aware of content personalization?

Yes ☐ No ☐

b) If yes, are you engaged in any content personalization activities?

Yes ☐ No ☐

c) If No, then we invite your preferences and opinions as follows:

(c.a) You are willing to personalize content because (Kindly choose the reason(s) from the ones listed below)

Large amounts of procured content are unused ☐

A small amount of acquired content is not being used properly ☐

Difficult to satisfy user demand otherwise ☐

Difficult to attract users otherwise ☐

Electronic content available can be easily personalized ☐

Leads to co-operative collection management ☐

Improves the image of Library ☐

Other Reasons (please specify) ☐

(c.b) You are not interested to personalize content because (Kindly choose the reason(s) from the ones listed below)

Importance not felt ☐

Lack of Infrastructure ☐

Inadequate Funds ☐

Lack of co-operation from management ☐

Inadequate Staff ☐

(c.c) If you are interested to personalize content and have not done so far, list the reasons:

d) If you are involved in content personalization, please list the type of personalization you have achieved with your library content:

List the activities you are focusing on right now:

e) Select the following benefits of content personalization that interest you:

Pin-pointed provision of information to users ☐

Users exposed to highly relevant content ☐

Users need to scan only a portion of the collection ☐

Library collection put to better use ☐

Improved collection development policies ☐

Enhanced use of library content ☐

Co-operative Collection Management ☐

Staff Training ☐

Others (please specify) ☐

f) How can CAS and SDI techniques be extended to content personalization?

Mention the tools and techniques used for content personalization:

g) Have you got a separate section/division in library to provide content personalization services?

Yes ☐ No ☐

If no, in which section are the activities conducted:

Acquisition ☐ Processing ☐

Reference ☐ Journals ☐

Computers ☐ Others (please specify)

h) Indicate the hardware used for content personalization:

Unix Servers ☐ NT Servers ☐

NT Workstations ☐ Multimedia PCs ☐

PCs ☐ VT100 Terminal ☐

Any other (please specify)

i) Indicate the software used for content personalization:

Operating System ☐

Library Automation Software ☐

Word Processing ☐ Database software ☐

Networking Software ☐ Multimedia ☐

Any other (please specify)

j) Indicate the content used for personalization (Give details)

Printed ☐

Electronic ☐

Book floppies/CDs ☐

Bibliographic databases ☐

Full text databases ☐

Electronic journals ☐

Internet/Web resources ☐

k) The personalized contents are provided:

In print format ☐ In electronic form ☐

Over LAN ☐ Through email ☐

Through website ☐

Any other (please specify)

l) Indicate the strength of the library staff for content personalization (please specify in numbers)

Dy. Librarians ☐ Asst. Librarians ☐

System Analysts ☐ STA ☐

TA ☐ Mechanics ☐

Clerical ☐ Attendants ☐

Support ☐ Others (please specify)

m) Mention the percentage of budget spent on content personalization:

n) In your opinion the budget spent on content personalization products and services is:

More than appropriate ☐

Appropriate ☐

Less than appropriate ☐

o) Preliminary data for content personalization has been collected based on:

Online/offline forms ☐

(Library usage history based on) Books issued ☐

Books requested ☐

Articles photocopied ☐

Articles referred ☐

Using Artificial Intelligence to auto-learn and intelligently refine the user's specialization

Any other (give details) ☐

p) In your opinion, content personalization must involve the following:

Content management ☐ Data mining ☐

Use characteristics ☐ Data intelligence ☐

**17. IMPACT OF CONTENT PERSONALIZATION**

In your view, what impact would content personalization have on:

a. Library Professionals

Day-to-day work:

Positive ☐ Negative ☐

Nil ☐

Efficiency:

Positive ☐ Negative ☐

Nil ☐

Productivity:

Positive ☐ Negative ☐

Nil ☐

b. Library Users

Meeting information needs:

Positive ☐ Negative ☐

Nil ☐

Relation with library:

Positive ☐ Negative ☐

Nil ☐

c. Information Organization

Collection development:

Positive ☐ Negative ☐

Nil ☐

Information processing:

Positive ☐ Negative ☐

Nil ☐

d. Information Services

Quality:

Positive ☐ Negative ☐

Nil ☐

Quantity:

Positive ☐ Negative ☐

Nil ☐

e. Library as a Whole

Library usage:

Positive ☐ Negative ☐

Nil ☐

Image:

Positive ☐ Negative ☐

Nil ☐

Technology adoption:

Positive ☐ Negative ☐

Nil ☐

Sociocultural impact:

Positive ☐ Negative ☐

Nil ☐

**18. EFFECT OF CONTENT PERSONALIZATION**

What effect do you think Content Personalization would have on the following library functions?

Library Services:

Improve ☐ Don't improve ☐

Remain the same ☐

User Satisfaction:

Improve ☐ Don't improve ☐

Remain the same ☐

Meeting User Demands:

Improve ☐ Don't improve ☐

Remain the same ☐

Library Material Usage:

Improve ☐ Don't improve ☐

Remain the same ☐

Library Image:

Improve ☐ Don't improve ☐

Remain the same ☐

**19. FUTURE PLANS**

What are the future plans for personalizing content in your library?

Kindly include any information on Content Personalization that you would like to add

Please mention the problems faced by you in personalizing content:

Please give your suggestions and solutions with regard to the above problems:

**Name of the person who filled up the questionnaire:**

**Designation:**

**Affiliation:**

Thank you for sparing valuable time to fill up this questionnaire and sharing your experiences for enhancing the utility of this study.

# Annexure 2
# Tables used in SAI

| Tables in SAI |
|---|
| book_emp |
| books |
| jour_emp |
| journals |
| login |
| news |
| news_emp |
| pdetails |
| per_emp |
| personal |
| sterms |
| sterms_emp |

**Login Table:**

| *Field* | *Type* | *Null* | *Default* |
|---|---|---|---|
| usrname | varchar(20) | YES | NULL |
| psswrd | varchar(36) | YES | NULL |
| empcode | varchar(15) | YES | NULL |

Example for Login Table:

| *usrname* | *psswrd* | *empcode* |
|---|---|---|
| gbandyo | ************************ | aerogb |
| rkumar | *********************** | ecerk |
| pkdatta | *********************** | aeropk |
| akgosh | *********************** | aeroakg |

**Pdetails Table:**

| *Field* | *Type* | *Null* | *Default* |
|---|---|---|---|
| empcode | varchar(15) | YES | NULL |
| name | varchar(30) | YES | NULL |
| email | varchar(50) | YES | NULL |
| dept | varchar(80) | YES | NULL |
| phone | varchar(15) | YES | NULL |

Example for Pdetails Table:

| *empcode* | *name* | *email* | *dept* | *phone* |
|---|---|---|---|---|
| bioamit | Das A K | amitk@hijli.iitkgp.ernet.in | Biotechnology | +91-3222-28356 |
| biodas | Das D | ddas@hijli.iitkgp.ernet.in | Biotechnology | +91-3222-283758 |

```
— MySQL dump 8.22
—
— Host: localhost    Database: sai
---------------------------------------------------------
— Server version                              3.23.54
—
— Table structure for table 'pdetails'
—
CREATE TABLE pdetails (
empcode varchar(15) default NULL,
name varchar(30) default NULL,
email varchar(50) default NULL,
dept varchar(80) default NULL,
phone varchar(15) default NULL
) TYPE=MyISAM;
—
— Dumping data for table 'pdetails'
—
```

INSERT INTO pdetails VALUES ('aerogb','Bandyopadhyay G','gbandyo@aero.iitkgp.ernet.in','Aerospace Engineering','+91-3222-283000');

INSERT INTO pdetails VALUES ('aeropk','Dutta P K','pkdatta@aero.iitkgp.ernet.in','Aerospace Engineering','91-3222-283002');

INSERT INTO pdetails VALUES ('aeroakg','Ghosh A K','akgosh@aero.iitkgp.ernet.in','Aerospace Engineering','91-3222-283004');

**Journal Table:**

| *Field* | *Type* | *Null* | *Default* |
|---|---|---|---|
| jcode | varchar(5) | YES | NULL |
| jname | varchar(100) | YES | NULL |
| jlink | text | YES | NULL |
| dept | varchar(30) | YES | NULL |

```
— MySQL dump 8.22
—
— Host: localhost    Database: sai
---------------------------------------------------------
— Server version                                3.23.54
—
— Table structure for table 'journals'
—
CREATE TABLE journals (
jcode varchar(5) default NULL,
jname varchar(100) default NULL,
jlink text,
dept varchar(30) default NULL
) TYPE=MyISAM;
—
— Dumping data for table 'journals'
—
```

INSERT INTO journals VALUES ('j1','ECE journals in IITKGP Library','http://www.library.iitkgp.ernet.in/usr/jnl/jleec.htm','ece');

INSERT INTO journals VALUES ('j2','Locations of Journals and Magazines','http://www.cs.columbia.edu/~hgs/netbib/where.html',NULL);

**Jour_emp Table** (Relation between journal and empcode):

| *Field* | *Type* | *Key* | *Default* |
|---|---|---|---|
| jcode | varchar(6) | YES | NULL |
| empcode | varchar(15) | YES | NULL |

```
— MySQL dump 8.22
—
— Host: localhost    Database: sai
————————————————————————————————————
— Server version                    3.23.54
—
— Table structure for table 'jour_emp'
—
CREATE TABLE jour_emp (
jcode varchar(6) default NULL,
empcode varchar(15) default NULL
) TYPE=MyISAM;
—
— Dumping data for table 'jour_emp'
—
INSERT INTO jour_emp VALUES ('j6'.'aerogb');
INSERT INTO jour_emp VALUES ('j46','eceswapna');
INSERT INTO jour_emp VALUES ('j3'.'ecerk');
```

**Books Table:**

| *Field* | *Type* | *Null* | *Default* |
|---|---|---|---|
| bcode | varchar(5) | YES | NULL |
| bname | varchar(100) | YES | NULL |
| blink | text | YES | NULL |
| dept | varchar(50) | YES | NULL |

```
— MySQL dump 8.22
—
— Host: localhost    Database: sai
————————————————————————————————————————
— Server version                          3.23.54
—
— Table structure for table 'books'
—
CREATE TABLE books (
bcode varchar(5) default NULL,
bname varchar(100) default NULL,
blink text,
dept varchar(50) default NULL
) TYPE=MyISAM;
—
— Dumping data for table 'books'
—
INSERT INTO books VALUES ('b1','Online books for ECE','http://onlinebooks.library.upenn.edu/webbin/book/subjectstart?TK',NULL);
INSERT INTO books VALUES ('b2','Online books for Networking','http://linux.oreillynet.com/pub/q/networking_chapters',NULL);
```

INSERT INTO books VALUES ('b3','Dictionary of Technical terms for Aerospace Use','http://roland.lerc.nasa.gov/~dglover/dictionary//content.html',NULL);

**Book_emp Table** (Relation between books and empcode):

| *Field* | *Type* | *Null* | *Default* |
|---|---|---|---|
| bcode | varchar(6) | YES | NULL |
| empcode | varchar(15) | YES | NULL |

```
— MySQL dump 8.22
—
— Host: localhost    Database: sai
------------------------------------------------------------
— Server version                              3.23.54
—
— Table structure for table 'book_emp'
—
CREATE TABLE book_emp (
bcode varchar(6) default NULL,
empcode varchar(15) default NULL
) TYPE=MyISAM;
—
— Dumping data for table 'book_emp'
—
INSERT INTO book_emp VALUES ('b2','ecerk');
INSERT INTO book_emp VALUES ('b1','ecerk');
INSERT INTO book_emp VALUES ('b3','aerogb');
```

**News Table**:

| *Field* | *Type* | *Null* | *Default* |
|---|---|---|---|
| ncode | varchar(5) | YES | NULL |
| nname | varchar(200) | YES | NULL |
| nlink | text | YES | NULL |
| dept | varchar(50) | YES | NULL |

```
— MySQL dump 8.22
—
— Host: localhost    Database: sai
———————————————————————————————————
— Server version                    3.23.54
—
— Table structure for table 'news'
—
CREATE TABLE news (
ncode varchar(5) default NULL,
nname varchar(200) default NULL,
nlink text,
dept varchar(50) default NULL
) TYPE=MyISAM;
—
— Dumping data for table 'news'
—
INSERT INTO news VALUES ('n1','Science Daily(Electronics)','http://www.sciencedaily.com/odp/Top/Science/Technology/Electronics',NULL);
INSERT INTO news VALUES ('n2','Times of India','http://www.timesofindia.com/',NULL);
INSERT INTO news VALUES ('n3','Telegraph','http://www.telegraphindia.com/section/frontpage/index.asp',NULL);
```

INSERT INTO news VALUES ('n4','Eenadu','http:////www.eenadu.net/',NULL);

INSERT INTO news VALUES ('n5','Aerospace Technology Innovations','http://nctn.hq.nasa.gov/innovation/index.html',NULL);

**News_emp Table** (Relation between news and empcode):

| *Field* | *Type* | *Null* | *Default* |
|---|---|---|---|
| node | varchar(6) | YES | NULL |
| empcode | varchar(15) | YES | NULL |

— MySQL dump 8.22

—

— Host: localhost Database: sai

---

— Server version 3.23.54

—

— Table structure for table 'news_emp'

—

CREATE TABLE news_emp (
ncode varchar(6) default NULL,
empcode varchar(15) default NULL
) TYPE=MyISAM;

—

— Dumping data for table 'news_emp'

—

INSERT INTO news_emp VALUES ('n77','ecerk');
INSERT INTO news_emp VALUES ('n2','ecerk');
INSERT INTO news_emp VALUES ('n3','ecerk');
INSERT INTO news_emp VALUES ('n4','ecerk');
INSERT INTO news_emp VALUES ('n5','aerogb');

**Personal Table:**

| *Field* | *Type* | *Null* | *Default* |
|---|---|---|---|
| pcode | varchar(5) | YES | NULL |
| pname | varchar(200) | YES | NULL |
| plink | text | YES | NULL |
| dept | varchar(50) | YES | NULL |

**Per_emp Table** (Relation between personal and empcode):

| *Field* | *Type* | *Null* | *Default* |
|---|---|---|---|
| pcode | varchar(6) | YES | NULL |
| empcode | varchar(15) | YES | NULL |

```
— MySQL dump 8.22
—
— Host: localhost    Database: sai
-----------------------------------------------------------
— Server version                              3.23.54
—
— Table structure for table 'per_emp'
—
CREATE TABLE per_emp (
pcode varchar(6) default NULL,
empcode varchar(15) default NULL
) TYPE=MyISAM;
—
— Dumping data for table 'per_emp'
—
INSERT INTO per_emp VALUES ('n10','aeroakg');
INSERT INTO per_emp VALUES ('n7','aeroakg');
INSERT INTO per_emp VALUES ('n9','aeroakg');
```

INSERT INTO per_emp VALUES ('n7','aeropk');

**Sterms Table:**

| *Field* | *Type* | *Null* | *Default* |
|---|---|---|---|
| scode | varchar(5) | YES | NULL |
| sname | varchar(50) | YES | NULL |
| dept | varchar(50) | YES | NULL |

— MySQL dump 8.22

—

— Host: localhost Database: sai

---

— Server version 3.23.54

—

— Table structure for table 'sterms'

—

CREATE TABLE sterms (
scode varchar(5) default NULL,
sname varchar(50) default NULL,
dept varchar(50) default NULL
) TYPE=MyISAM;

—

— Dumping data for table 'sterms'

—

INSERT INTO sterms VALUES ('s1','Aerodynamics','Aerospace Engineering');

INSERT INTO sterms VALUES ('s2','Aeroelasticity','Aerospace Engineering');

INSERT INTO sterms VALUES ('s3','Aerospacestructures','Aerospace Engineering');

INSERT INTO sterms VALUES ('s4','Computer Networks'.'ece');

INSERT INTO sterms VALUES ('s5','Digital Signal Processing','ece');

**sterms_emp table** (Relation between search terms and empcode):

| *Field* | *Type* | *Null* | *Default* |
|---|---|---|---|
| scode | varchar(6) | YES | NULL |
| empcode | varchar(15) | YES | NULL |

```
— MySQL dump 8.22
—
— Host: localhost    Database: sai
————————————————————————————————————
— Server version                          3.23.54
—
— Table structure for table 'sterms_emp'
—
CREATE TABLE sterms_emp (
scode varchar(6) default NULL,
empcode varchar(15) default NULL
) TYPE=MyISAM;
—
— Dumping data for table 'sterms_emp'
—
INSERT INTO sterms_emp VALUES ('s4','ecerk');
INSERT INTO sterms_emp VALUES ('s5','ecerk');
INSERT INTO sterms_emp VALUES ('s6','ecerk');
```

# Annexure 3
# SAI Feedback Form

Please complete this online form and help us improve the Service.

1. Can you tell us why you accessed this Service? (Check all that apply)

   To use INDEST Resources

   To use Library resources

   To use web resources

   Any other (please specify)

2. What are your information needs from this Service? (Check all that apply)

   Academic research

   Personal research

   Use as a teaching tool

   Any other (please specify)

3. How frequently are you using this Service?

   Daily once

   More than once a day

   Weekly once

   ___times a week

   Monthly once

   ___times a month

   Any other (please specify)

4. How would you rate your overall satisfaction with the Service?

   Very satisfied

   Satisfied

Neither satisfied nor dissatisfied

Dissatisfied

Very dissatisfied

5. Compared to available alternatives, the SAI Service is

   Much better

   Somewhat better

   About the same

   Inferior

6. What could be improved about this Service?

   Look and appearance

   Content

   Any other (please specify)

7. What did you like most about this Service?

8. What did you like least about this Service?

9. Will you use this Service again?

   Definitely yes

   Probably yes

   Might or might not

   Probably not

   Definitely not

10. Did you find what you were looking for?

    Yes No

    If no, what was it?

11. Did you find this Service easy to use?

    Yes No

    If no, please state why:

12. Do you think the SAI Service useful?

    Yes No

    If no, please state why:

13. How easy was it for you to find the information that you needed on the website?

    Couldn't find at all

    Very hard

    Hard

    Average

    Easy

    Very easy

14. How useful would you rate the Service overall?

    Not useful at all

    Not very useful

    Satisfactory

    Very useful

15. How reliable and trustworthy would you rate the information you find on this Service?

    Very reliable

    Somewhat reliable

    Somewhat unreliable

    Not at all reliable

16. How current and up-to-date would you rate the information you find on this Service?

    Very current and up-to-date

    New to me, but not necessarily new to others

    I read this the last time I looked at your site

17. Do you use the SAI website as the first online stop in your search for information in your specialization?

    Yes No

18. How important is it to you to be able to ask a question online to a professional?

    Very helpful

Helpful

Somewhat helpful

Not at all helpful

19. What other information would you like to see on this Service?

20. Have you ever recommended this Service to others?

    Yes No

    Not sure

21. Would you recommend this Service to a friend or colleague?

    Definitely yes

    Probably yes

    Might or might not

    Probably not

    Definitely not

22. Have you experienced any problems while using this Service?

23. How would you rate the search facility on this Service in terms of helping you find the information you were looking for?

24. Did you find the information provided on this Service easy to understand?

25. What other information would you like to see included on the Service?

26. Would you like to make any other comment on this Service?

27. Thank you for your time and feedback. This question is optional. However, it would be useful if you could give the following details to help us profile users:

    Name:

    Department:

    Email:

# General Bibliography

1. **Agarwal** (P K). India's National Internet Backbone. *Communications of ACM*. 42, 6; June 1999; 53-58.
2. **Allen** (T J). Organisational aspects of information flow in Technology. *Aslib Proceedings*. 20; 1968; 433-454.
3. **Allen** (R B), **Obry** (P) and **Littman** (M). An interface for navigating clustered document sets returned by queries. *Proceedings of the ACM Conference on Organizational Computing Systems*. 1993. p 166-171.
4. **American Chemical Society**. Will Science Publishing Perish? The paradox of contemporary journals. Washington.
5. **Anderson** (Dorothy). Universal Bibliographic Control. In Encyclopedia of Library and Information Science. 1984. V 37, Supplement 2. Marcel Dekker. New York. p 366-401.
6. **Andrews** (Chris). Understanding CD-ROM software. *CD-ROM Professional*. July 1990; 59-62.
7. **Arms** (William Y). Digital Libraries for Distance Education, Editorial. *D-Lib Magazine*. 6, 10; October 2000.
8. **Association of Research Libraries**. Definition and Purposes of a Digital Library, http:// sunsite.berkeley.edu/ ARL/definition.html, October 23, 1995, updated 1/10/96, (accessed on 06.12.2000)
9. **Atkins** (Helen). The ISI Web of Science - Links and Electronic Journals How links work today in the Web of Science, and the challenges posed by electronic journals. *D-Lib Magazine*. 5, 9; September 1999. DOI: 10.1045/ september99-atkins.
10. **Atkinson** (Randall J). Towards a More Secure Internet.

*IEEE Computer*. 30, 1; January 1997; 57-61.

11. **Au** (Ka-Neng). CD-ROM interoperability. *CD-ROM Librarian*. September 1992; 22-25.

12. **Balabanovic** (Marko) and **Shaham** (Yoav). Learning Information Retrieval Agents: Experiments with Automated Web Browsing. *Proceedings of the AAAI Spring Symposium Series on Information Gathering from Heterogeneous, Distributed Environments*. 1995. p 13-18

13. **Beagrie** (Neil) and **Greenstein** (Daniel). A Strategic Policy Framework for Creating and Preserving Digital Collections, Version 4.0, 14/7/98, Final Draft. *Internet Scout Review*. 5, 2; 8 May 1998. http://www.ukoln.ac.uk/services/ papers/bl/framework/framework.html

14. **Beebe** (Linda) and **Meyers** (Barbara). Digital Workflow: Managing the Process Electronically. *The Journal of Electronic Publishing*. 5, 4; June 2000. http://www.press.umich. edu/jep/05-04/sheridan.html

15. **Beebe** (Linda) and **Meyers** (Barbara). The Unsettled State of Archiving. *The Journal of Electronic Publishing*. 4, 4; June 1999. http://www.press.umich.edu/ jep/04-04/beebe.html

16. **Belkin** (N.J). Anomalous states of knowledge as a basis for information retrieval. *Canadian Journal of Information Science*. 5; 1980; 133-143.

17. **Belkin** (N) and **Croft** (W B). Information Filtering and Information Retrieval: Two Sides of the Same Coin. *Communications of the ACM*. 35, 12; 1992; 29-38.

18. **Berners-Lee** (Tim) *et al*. The World Wide Web. *Communications of the ACM*. 37, 8; August 1994; 76-82.

19. **Bernhadt** (Homer I). Engineering Libraries and Collections. In Encyclopedia of Library and Information Science. 1972. V 8. Marcel Dekker. New York. p 73.

20. **Bernstein** (Jerome S). Computers and Information

Systems. 1986. CBS College; Holt, Rinehart & Winston, New York.

21. **Binder** (Michael B). Licensing Models: Information as a Commodity. *The Journal of Electronic Publishing*. 3, 3; March 1998. http://www.press.umich.edu/ jep/03-03/binder.html

22. **Bishoff** (Liz). Interoperability and Standards in a Museum/Library Collaborative: The Colorado Digitization Project. *First Monday*. 5, 6; June 2000. http://firstmonday.org/issues/issue5_6/bishoff/

23. **Bogardus** (Janet). Business Libraries and Information Collections. In Encyclopedia of Library and Information Science. 1970V 3. Marcel Dekker. New York. p 530-553.

24. **Broadbent** (K P) and **Lafond** (R). The future of scientific, technical, and industrial information to third users-A donors view (The experiences of International Development Research Centre (IDRC), Canada). *International conference on documentation services in science, technology, and industry*. Leningrad, IAEA-SM-317/66. May 1990. p 28-31.

25. **Brophy** (P). Networking in British academic libraries. *British Journal of Academic Librarianship*. 8, 1; 1993; 49-60.

26. **Budington** (William S). Access to Information. In Advances in Librarianship. 1971. V 2. Seminar Press. New York. p 1-43.

27. **Bush** (V). As We May Think. *Atlantic Monthly*. 176, 1; 1945; 101-108.

28. **CPA** and **RLG**. Preserving Digital Information. Report of the Task Force on Archiving of Digital Information, commissioned by The Commission on Preservation and Access and The Research Libraries Group. May 1, 1996. http://www.rlg.org/ArchTF/tfadi.recommen.htm #practices

29. **Carbonell** (J G) and Hood (G). The World Modelers Project: Objectives and simulator architecture. *In* Michalsi (R S), Carbonell (J G) and Mitchells (T M), *Ed.* Machine Learning: A guide to current research. 1986. Kluwer. Boston, MA.

30. **Casey-Cohen** (Lorna). Significance of Law Library Value Added Services in the1990's Law Firm. http://www.llrx.com/features/lorna.htm (accessed on 15.12.2000).

31. **Casado** (Margaret). Delivering library services to remote students. *Computers in Libraries*. 21, 4; April 2001; 32-38.

32. **Chakraborty** (Arun Kumar). Publishing on CD-ROM: Indian Potential. *DESIDOC Bulletin of Information Technology*. 17, 5; September1997; 23-31.

33. **Chapman** (Stephen) and **Kenney** (Anne R). Digital Conversion of Research Library Materials: A Case for Full Informational Capture. *D-Lib Magazine*. October 1996. http://www.dlib.org/dlib/october96/cornell/10chapman.html

34. **Chen** (Ching - Chih). Scientific and Technical Information. 1977. MIT Press. Cambridge, Mass.

35. **Chen** (H) and **Dumais** (S T). Bringing order to the web: Automatically categorizing search results. *Proceedings of CHI'00, Human Factors in Computing Systems*. 2000. p 145-152.

36. **Cheng** (Y) and **Fu** (K). Conceptual clustering in knowledge organization. *IEEE Transactions on Pattern Analysis and Machine Intelligence*. 7; 1985; 592-598.

37. **Choudhury** (G. Sayeed) *et al.* Digital Workflow Management: The Lester S. Levy Digitized Collection of Sheet Music. *First Monday*. 5, 6; June 2000. http://www.firstmonday.org/issues/ issue5_6/choudhury/

38. **Chowdhury** (G G) and Chowdhury (Sudatta). Text retrieval and library management software in India. *Program*. 28, 3; July 1994; 253-261.
39. **Cochrane** (Pauline A). Can a standard for an online Common Command Language be developed? *Online*. January 1983; 36-37.
40. **Coffman** (Steve). Distance education and virtual reference: Where are we headed. *Computers in Libraries*. 21, 4; April 2001; 20-25.
41. **Communications of the ACM**, Special Issues of April 1995, August 1995, April 1998.
42. **Compton** (Dale W). Engineering Management, Creating and Managing World-Class Operations. Prentice Hall. New Jersey. p 372.
43. **Crouse** (Maurice). Citing Electronic Information in History Papers. 19 February 2001. http://www.people.memphis.edu/~mcrouse/elcite.html (accessed on 21 May 2001)
44. **Cuadra** (Carlos A). Online systems: Promises and pitfalls. *Journal of the American Society for Information Science*. March-April 1971; 107-114.
45. **Cutting** (D R), **Karger** (D R). **Pedersen**, (J O), and **Tukey** (J W). Scatter/Gather: a cluster-based approach to browsing large document collections. *Proceedings of the International ACM SIGIR Conference on Research and Development in information Retrieval*, 15th. 1992. p 318-329.
46. **Debons** (Anthony) *et al.* Information Science: An integrated view. 1989. G K Hall. p 1-19.
47. **Deerwester** (S), **Dumais** (S T), **Furnas** (G W), **Landauer** (T K) and **Harshman** (R). Indexing by Latent Semantic Analysis. *Journal of the American Society for Information Science*. 41, 6; 1990; 391-407.

48. **DELNET Newsletter**, different issues.

49. **Dempsey** (Kathy (Miller)). Reaching faraway patrons, editor's notes. *Computers in Libraries*. 21, 4; April 2001; 6.

50. **Department of Science and Technology**, Government of India. Science & Technology Pocket Data Book. 1992. DST. New Delhi.

51. **Dhaka** (R P S) and Arora (Kamlesh). Privatization of S & T Information Services- The INSDOC Experience. *DESIDOC Bulletin of Information Technology*. 15, 5; September1995; 7-10.

52. Digital Library Initiatives, Building Digital Libraries: Digital Library Projects, The University of Texas at Austin Library Online. June 7, 2001. http://www.lib.utexas.edu/dli/digital.html (accessed on 04.08.2001)

53. **Dikshit** (Sandeep). Growth in Internet Connections Lopsided. *The Hindu*. Visakhapatnam. December 10, 2000.

54. **Dublin Core Qualifiers**. 2000-07-11. http://dublincore.org/documents/dcmes-qualifiers/ (accessed on 5 June 2001)

55. **Emerald Consortia**. http://www.emeraldinsight.com/consortia/

56. **Etzioni** (O) and **Perkowitz** (M). Adaptive Web Sites: an AI Challenge. *Proceedings of the Fifteenth International Joint Conference on Artificial Intelligence*. 1997.

57. **Fleischhauer** (Carl). Digital Formats for Content Reproductions. July 13, 1998. http://memory.loc.gov/ammem/formats.html#VIII

58. **Forbes** (Judith L). Perspectives on Lifelong Learning: The View from a Distance. *First Monday*. 5, 11; November 2000. http://firstmonday.org/issues/issue5_11/ forbes/index.html

59. **Fox** (Edward A) *et al.* National Digital Library of Theses

and Dissertations: A Scalable and Sustainable Approach to Unlock University Resources. *D-Lib Magazine*. September 1996. http://www.dlib.org/dlib/september96/theses/09fox. html

60. **French** (James C) and **Viles** (Charles L). Personalized Information Environments: An Architecture for Customizable Access to Distributed Digital Libraries. *D-Lib Magazine*. 5, 6; June 1999.

61. **Gatenby** (Janifer). Internet, Interoperability and Standards – Filling the Gaps. http://www.niso.org/Gatenby.html

62. **Ghosh** (Anindo). Internet Bandwidth: India Needs a Backbone. http://www.ieo.org/backbone.html (accessed on 10.12.2000)

63. **Goel** (Lt. Mohit) and **Sarkar** (Sudeshna). Web Site Personalization By Learning User Profile. *Proceedings of IMeL 2002*. Allied. New Delhi.

64. **Greenspun** (Philip). Internet Application Workbook. http://philip.greenspun.com/ internet-application-workbook/content-management (accessed on 08 July 2001)

65. **Grenquist** (Peter). Why I Don't Read Electronic Journals: An Iconoclast Speaks Out. *The Journal of Electronic Publishing*. 3, 1; September 1997. http://www.press.umich.edu/jep/ 03-01/Iconoclast.html

66. **Griffith** (C). Five advantages of electronic books. *Information Today*. 12, 3; Mar 1995; 10-11.

67. **Grogan** (Denis). Science and Technology: An introduction to literature. 3rd rev. ed. 1976. Clive Bingley. London.

68. **Guenther** (Kim). Designing and managing your digital library. *Computers in Libraries*. 20, 1; 2000; 34-39.

69. **Hammer** (Sebastian) and **Favaro** (John). Z39.5 and the World Wide Web. *Dlib Magazine*. March 1996. http://www.dlib.org/dlib/march96/briefings/03indexdata. html

70. **Haynes** (David) *et al.* Responsibility for digital archiving

and long term access to digital data. http://www.ukoln.ac.uk/services/papers/bl/jisc-npo67/digital-preservation.html

71. **Hedstrom** (Margaret) and **Montgomery** (Sheon). Digital Preservation Needs and Requirements in RLG Member Institutions. A study commissioned by the Research Libraries Group. December 1998. http://www.rlg.org/preserv/digpres. html

72. **Helling** (Bill). Web-site sensitivity to privacy concerns: Collecting Personally Identifiable Information and Passing Persistent Cookies. *First Monday*. 3, 2; 1998. http://www.firstmonday.org/issues/issue3_2/helling/index.html#author

73. **Helmer** (John F). Editorial: Epidemiology of the Consortial Spore. *Information Technology and Libraries*. 18, 3; Sept 1999.

74. **Henry** (W M) *et al.* Online searching. 1982. Butterworths. London.

75. **Hodge** (Gail M). An Information Life-Cycle Approach: Best Practices for Digital Archiving. *The Journal of Electronic Publishing*. 5, 4; June 2000. http://www.press.umich.edu/ jep/05-04/hodge.html

76. **Hertz** (D B) and **Rubenstein** (A H). Team Research. New York, Columbia University, Dept. of Industrial Engineering. 1954 (cited in Lancaster (F W). Towards Paperless Information Systems. 1978. Academic Press. New York).

77. **Hirshon** (Arnold) *et al.* International Coalition of Library Consortia (ICOLC) Statement of Current Perspective and Preferred Practices for the Selection and Purchase of Electronic Information. http://www.library.yale.edu/consortia/ statement.html

78. **Hooke** (Julie). Distance Education: The Perils of the Virtual Student in Cyberspace. *The Journal of Electronic*

*Publishing*. 5, 1; September 1999. http://www.press.umich.edu/jep/05-01/hooke.html

79. http://sunsite.berkeley.edu/ARL/definition.html (accessed on 06.12.2000)
80. http://www.iitd.ac.in/new/knet.html
81. http://www.informindia.com (accessed on 26.12.2000)
82. http://www.insdoc.org, follow the link 'Services, Products & Publications' (accessed on 10.12.2000)
83. www.krdl.org.sg/General/PressClips/nlb.html (accessed on 15.12.2000).
84. **Hughes** (Carol Ann). Lessons Learned: Digitization of Special Collections at The University of Iowa Libraries. *D-Lib Magazine*. 6, 6; June 2000. http://www.dlib.org/dlib/june00/hughes/06hughes.html
85. **IEEE Computer**. May 1996.
86. **International Coalition of Library Consortia (ICOLC)**. Statement of Current Perspective and Preferred Practices for the Selection and Purchase of Electronic Information. Update No. 1. New Developments In E-Journal Licensing. (December 2001 update to March 1998 Statement), http://www.library.yale.edu/consortia/2001currentpractices.htm
87. **International Federation of Library Associations and Institutions** (http://www.nlc-bnc.ca/ifla/I/training/listserv/lists.htm)
88. **Ishii** (Kei) and **Lutterbeck** (Bernd). Unexploited Resources of Online Education for Democracy - Why the Future Should Belong to OpenCourseWare. *First Monday*. 6, 11; November 2001. http://firstmonday.org/issues/issue6_11/ishii/ index.html
89. **Jeffrey** (Dean) and **Henzinger** (Monika R). Finding related pages in the World Wide Web. *Proceedings of the International World Wide Web Conference, 8th* Toronto,

Canada, May 1999. Elsevier Science. p 389-401.

90. **Ladendorf** (Janice M). Information Flow in Science, Technology, and Commerce. *Special Libraries*. 61; 1970; 215-222.

91. **Jeevan** (V K J) and **Padhi** (P). Towards Personalising the Electronic Contents in Technical Libraries. *University News*. 40; 21; May 27- June 2 2002; p 3-9.

92. **Jeevan** (V K J) and **Padhi** (P). Standardizing Subject Term Assignment for a Library Personalization System. Second International Convention on Automation of Libraries in Education and Research Institutions (CALIBER) 2004, New Delhi, 11-13 February 2004. In Proceedings Volume. 2004. Information and Library Network (INFLIBNET) Centre. Ahmedabad. p 312-320.

93. **Jeevan** (V K J) and **Padhi** (P). Personalizing INDEST Contents in IITs: Options and Benefits. Society for Information Science (SIS) 2003 Conference, Roorkee, 9-11 April 2003. In Conference Volume. 2003. Central Library, IIT Roorkee. Roorkee. p. 683-693.

94. **Jeevan** (V K J) and **Padhi** (P). User Interest Management for Personalizing Electronic Contents in IITs. National Convention on Library and Information Networking (NACLIN) 2003 Conference, Jadavpur, 14-17 October 2003. In Conference Volume. 2003. DELNET. Delhi. p 251-264.

95. **Jeevan** (V K J) and **Padhi** (P). Library Personalization: Avenues for IITs. SIS 2004 Conference, Chennai, 22-23 January 2004. In Conference Volume. 2004. Central Library, IIT Madras. Chennai. p 499-507.

96. **Jones** (R C) *et al.* Keeping Up to Date and Solving Problems in Engineering. *Proceedings of the World Conference on Continuing Engineering Education*. 1986. IEEE. New York. p 784-791.

97. **Jonker** (Frederick). The new 'Termatrex' line of IR systems - the minimatrex line of IR systems. *American Documentation*. 14, 4; 1963; 276-282.

98. **Journal Citation Reports** (JCR) on CD-ROM - 1999 Science Edition, Philadelphia: Institute for Scientific Information.

99. **Kalseth** (Karl). Knowledge Management from a Business Strategy Perspective. *FID Review*. 1, 1; 1999; 37-41.

100. **Katz** (Donald L) and **Tucker** (Stanley A). Engineering Literature. In Encyclopedia of Library and Information Science. 1972. V 8. Marcel Dekker. New York. p 91.

101. **Katz** (William A). Introduction to Reference Work: Vol 1, Basic Information Sources. 1969. McGraw Hill. New York. p 98.

102. **Kaul** (H K). DELNET: the first operational library network in India. *DESIDOC Bulletin of Information Technology*. 16, 2; 1996; 23-34.

103. **Kay** (John). Foundations of Corporate Success: How Business Strategies Add Value. 1993. OUP. New York. p 19-30.

104. **Kies** (Cosette). Problems in Library Public Relations. 1974. R R Bowker. New York. xiv+179 p.

105. **Kohonen** (T). In Shavlik (J W) and Dietterich (T G), *Ed*. Readings in Machine Learning. 1982. Morgan Kaufmann. San Mateo, CA.

106. **Kramer** (Joseph) *et al.* A User-Centered Design Approach to Personalization. Communications of ACM. 43, 8; August 2000; 45-48.

107. **Kroeber** (Donald W) and **Watson** (Hugh J). Computer based Information Systems: A Management Approach. 1984. Macmillan. New York.

108. **Kumar** (Pramod) and **Arora** (O P). Information and Library Network (INFLIBNET) Programme. *Desidoc*

*Bulletin of Information Technology* (DBIT). 16, 2; March 1996; 11-22.

109. **Kumar** (Pramod) and **Kumbar** (T S). INFLIBNET Activities: Status, Plans and Strategies for the future. *Proceedings of CALIBER 98, Information Management in Academic and Research Libraries*. 1998. INFLIBNET Centre. Ahmedabad. p 249-257.

110. **Lahiri** (Abhijit). Information Market Scenario in India. *Information Today & Tomorrow*. 15, 1; Jan-March 1996; 17-30.

111. **Lahiri** (Abhijit) and **Singh** (B G Sunder). Experiences of Library Network Development in India. 1998. *Key Note Address in CALIBER 98*. Bhubaneswar.

112. **Landesman** (M) and **van Reenen** (J). Consortia vs. reform: creating congruence. *JEP: the Journal of Electronic Publishing*. 6, 2; Dec 2000. http://www.press.umich.edu/ jep/06-02/landesman.html

113. **Larson** (Ray R). Search Capabilities for Users of Digital Libraries: Tools and Paradigms. http://is.gseis.ucla.edu/research/dl/larson.html (accessed on 06.12.2000)

114. **Lawrence** (David B). The Economic Value of Information. 1999. Springer. New York. p300.

115. **Levy** (D M). Fixed or Fluid? Document Stability and New Media. *Proceedings of ECHT'94*. Edinburgh, Sept. 18-23. 1994. ACM. New York. p 24-31 (cited in **Levy** (David M) and Marshall (Catherine C). "Going Digital: Assumptions underlying Digital Libraries". *Communications of the ACM*. 38, 4; April 1995; 78)

116. **Lewin** (K). Group decision and social change. *In* Maccoby *et al. Ed*. Readings in Social Psychology. Holt. New York. p 197-211.

117. **Lieberman** (H). Letizia: An agent that assists web browsing. *International Joint Conference of Artificial Intelligence*. Aug.1995. Montreal.

118. **Luhn** (H P). Selective dissemination of new scientific information with the aid of electronic processing equipment. *American Documentation*. 12, 1; 1961; 131-138.

119. **Lynch** (Clifford) and **Garcia-Molina** (Hector). Interoperability, Scaling, and the Digital Libraries Research Agenda: A Report on the May 18-19, 1995, IITA Digital Libraries Workshop. August 22, 1995. http://www.itrd.gov/pubs/iita-dlw/main.html (accessed on 05.12.2000)

120. **Machlup** (Fritz). The production and distribution of knowledge in the United States. 1962. University Press. Princeton.

121. **Mann** (Steve). Computer Architectures for Personal Space: Forms-Based Reasoning in the Domain of Humanistic Intelligence. *First Monday*. 6, 8; August 2001. URL: http://firstmonday.org/issues/issue6_8/mann/ index.html

122. **Marcus** (J). Extremely local news: community newspapers on the Web. *Database*. 21, 2; Apr/May 1998; 73-75.

123. **Mashelkar** (R A). Convocation Address. 2000. IIT Kharagpur.

124. **MIT**. MIT OpenCourseWare Factsheet. http://web.mit.edu/newsoffice/ nr/2001/ocw-facts.html

125. **McGarry** (K J). The changing context of information: An introductory analysis. 1981. Clive Bingley. London. p 11-36.

126. **Miller** (Dick R) and **Buttner** (Mary). Digital Materials: Cost and Access Issues. 31 January 2001. www.med.stanford.edu/lane/general/publishing/dmissues.html (accessed on 15 June 2001).

127. **Miller** (Robert C) and **Bharat** (Krishna). SPHINX: a framework for creating personal, site-specific web crawlers. *Proceedings of the International World Wide*

*Web Conference*. 7th, Brisbane, Australia. Elsevier Science. April 1998. p 119-130.

128. **Mischo** (William H) and **Lee** (Jounghyoun). End-user searching of bibliographic databases. *Annual Review of Information Science and Technology*. 22; 1987; 227-263.

129. **Mitra** (A C). CALIBNET on stream. *DESIDOC Bulletin of Information Technology*. 16, 2; 1996; 35-40.

130. **Moffat** (M). An EEVL solution to engineering information on the Internet. *Aslib Proceedings*. 48, 6; Jun 1996; 147-150.

131. **Moore** (Frazier H). Public Relations Principles, Cases and Problems. 1981. Richard D. Irwin. Homewood. 8th ed. p 5.

132. **Moore** (Reagan) *et al.* Collection-Based Persistent Digital Archives - Part 1. *D-Lib Magazine*. 6, 3; March 2000. http://www.dlib.org/dlib/march00/moore/ 03moore-pt1.html

133. **Mühlberger** (Günter). Digitization of Printed Material: The METAe Project. *D-Lib Magazine*. 7, 3; March 2001. http://www.dlib.org/dlib/march01/03inbrief.html#MUEHLBERGER

134. **Najork** (Marc) and **Wiener** (Janet). Breadth-first search crawling yields high quality pages. *Proceedings of the International World Wide Web Conference*. 10th, May 2001, Hong Kong, China. ACM Press. p 114-118.

135. **Newnes Communication Technology Handbook**. 1994. Butterworth Hienemann. p 53-56.

136. **Noerr** (Peter). The Digital Library Toolkit. 2[nd] ed. March 2000. Sun Microsystems. Palo Alto. http://www.sun.com/products-n-solutions/edu/libraries/ digitaltoolkit.html, (accessed on 04.12.2000).

137. **O'Hagan** (M). Translating in cyberspace: the coming industry of teletranslation. *Aslib Proceedings*. 47, 2; Feb 1995; 41-46.

138. **Pace** (Andrew K). Distance learning services; It's closer than you think. *Computers in Libraries*. 21, 4; April 2001; 49-51.

139. **Pai** (Uday Lal). India's Bandwidth Dilemma (in 2 parts), http://www.newmedia.com/nm-article-2294.asp and http://www.newmedia.com/ nm-article-2318.asp (accessed on 11.12.2000)

140. **Pazzani** (M), **Maramatsu** (J) and **Billsus** (D). Syskill & webert: Identifying interesting web sites. *Proceedings of AAAI conference*. 1996. Portland.

141. **Penland** (Patrick R). Content Analysis. In Encyclopedia of Library and Information Science. 1971. V 5. Marcel Dekker. New York. p 633.

142. **Perone** (Karen). Networking of CD-ROMs: A Tutorial Introduction. CD-ROM Librarian. February 1996; 71-77.

143. **Phillips** (Margaret E). Ensuring Long-Term Access to Online Publications. http://www.press.umich.edu/jep/04-04/phillips.html (accessed on 10 July 2001)

144. **Prasad** Ravi Visvesvaraya. Paranoia in Gigabytes. The Telegraph, Calcutta. XIX, 1; July 7, 2000; 10.

145. **Price** (Derek J. De Solla). Little Science Big Science. 1963. Columbia University Press New York. p 118.

146. **Price** (Derek J. De Solla). Measuring the Size of Science. *Proc. Israel Acad. Sciences and Humanities*. 4, 6; 1989; p 98-111.

147. **Raghavan** (R) and Raghavan (J). Notable features of MALIBNET. *DESIDOC Bulletin of Information Technology*. 16, 2; 1996; p 47-56.

148. **Rajashekar** (T B). CD-ROM Retrieval engines. *Workshop on CD-ROM technology*. NAL, Bangalore. 16-18 November 1993. p 8.

149. **Rajashekar** (T B). What's new in Computers? Digital Libraries. *Resonance*. April 1997; p 60-73.

150. **Ramani** (S). Report from the Bombay Library Network. *DESIDOC Bulletin of Information Technology*. 16, 2; March 1996; p 41-46.

151. **Ranganathan**, (S R). Prolegomena to Library Classification. SRELS. Bangalore. 3rd ed. 1994. p 490.

152. **Ravi** (A S). An overview of existing CD-ROM standards. *National meet on CD-ROM/online users*. 3rd, NICLAI, Madras. 9-10 August 1994. p 11.

153. **Ray** (Kathryn) and **Day** (Joan). Student attitudes towards electronic information resources. http://InformationR.net/ir/4-2/paper54.html (accessed on 9 July 2001)

154. **Renborg** (Greta). Library Public Relations. In Encyclopedia of Library and Information Science. 1984 V 37. Marcel Dekker. New York. p 238-239.

155. **Revill** (Don H). Performance Measures for Academic Libraries. In Encyclopedia of Library and Information Science. 1990. V 45 (Sup. 10). Marcel Dekker. New York. p 306-309.

156. **Richards** (Trevor) and **Robinson** (Christine). Evaluating CD-ROM software: A model. *CD-ROM Professiona*. September 1993; 92-101.

157. **Salton** (G). The state of retrieval system evaluation. *Information processing & Management*. 8, 4; 1992; 441.

158. **Scully** (Paul). Internet: a Core or Value Added Service? A Discussion Paper, Public Libraries Branch, September 1997. http://www.slnsw.gov.au/plb/ publish/interacc/summd.htm (accessed on 15.12.2000).

159. **Shklar** (Leon). Advanced Web Presentation through Data Modeling An Open Architecture for the Personalized Webs of the Future. *D-Lib Magazine*. April 1996.

160. **Singh** (B G Sunder). Indigenous databases and information products/services. *Information Today and Tomorrow* (NISSAT Newsletter). April-June 1997; p 22-25.

161. **Smith** (Gerald F). Managerial Problem Solving. In Encyclopedia of Library and Information Science. 1994. V 53. Marcel Dekker. New York. p 210-236.

162. **Smith** (Natalia). UNC-CH Library Digitization Project "Documenting the American South: The Southern Experience in 19th-Century America". *D-Lib Magazine*. Clips and Pointers, November 1997. http://www.dlib.org/dlib/ november97/11clips.html#UNC

163. **Srinivasan** (M R). Misuse of Science. *The Hindu*. 16 August, 2000. p12.

164. **Srinivasan** (Padmini). Digital Library Projects in the United States. *DESIDOC Bulletin of Information Technology*. 17, 6; November1997; 15-21.

165. **Stanford Digital Library Technologies**. http://www-diglib.stanford.edu/diglib/index.html/ (accessed on 04.12.2000)

166. **Stonebraker** (Michael) and **Hellerstein** (Joseph M). Content Integration for E-business. http://db.cs.berkeley.edu/~jmh/miscpapers/sigmod-content.pdf (accessed on 15 July 2001)

167. **Subramanyam** (K). Scientific Literature. In Encyclopedia of Library and Information Science. 1979. V 26. Marcel Dekker. New York. p 382, 391, 392, 394, 396, 400, 433.

168. **Subramanyam** (K). Technical Literature. In Encyclopedia of Library and Information Science. 1980. V 30. Marcel Dekker. New York. p 144-209.

169. **Sur** (S N) and **Singh** (B G Sunder). Indian Abstracting & Indexing Services in Science & Technology. *Information Today & Tomorrow*. 14, 1; Jan-March 1995; 11-24.

170. **Stear** (E B). Technology-enabled content: threat or opportunity? *Online*. 21, 4; July/August 1997; 80-82.

171. **Taylor** (R S). Question negotiation and information seeking in libraries. *College and Research Libraries*. 28; 1968; 178-194.

172. **Tedd** (Lucy A). An introduction to sharing resources via the Internet in academic libraries and information centres in Europe. *Program*. January 1995; 43-61.

173. The Association of Research Libraries, the American Association of Law Libraries, the American Library Association, the Association of Academic Health Sciences Library Directors, the Medical Library Association, the Special Libraries Association and the Art Libraries Society of North America, **Fair Use in the Electronic Age: Serving the Public Interest** (Jan 18, 1995). http://arl/cni.org/scomm/copyright/uses.html

174. **Thibadeau** (Robert) and **Benoit** (Evan). Antique Books. *D-Lib Magazine*. September 1997. http://www.dlib.org/dlib/september97/thibadeau/09thibadeau. html

175. **Toub** (S E). Adding value to Internet collections. *Library Hi Tech*. 15, 3-4; 1997; 148-154.

176. **LaQuey** (Tracy) and **Ryer** (Jeanne C). The Internet Companion: A Beginner's Guide To Global Networking. The Online BookStore Edition. 1992. Addison-Wesley.

177. **UNESCO**. MOST Clearing House Best Practices. http://www.unesco.org/most/ bphome.htm

178. **UNESCO**. Statistical Year Book 1996. 1997. Bernan Press. Lanham: p 7-44.

179. **Vetter** (Ronald J) *et al.* Mosaic and the World Wide Web. *IEEE Computer*. October 1994; 49-57.

180. **Vickery** (Brian). A century of Scientific and Technical Information. *Journal of Documentation*. 55, 5; 1999; 476-527.

181. **Vijayakumar** (K P). Developments in the Indian telecom sector: implications for libraries and information centers. *Library Science with a Slant to Documentation and Information Studies*. 34, 4; Dec 1997; 173-183.

182. **Voight** (Melvin J). Scientist's Approaches to Information.

ACRL Monograph 24. American Library Association. 1961. p 20-33.

183. **Warnick** (Walter L). First Personalized Alert Service for Preprints. In Brief. *D-Lib Magazine*. 6, 12; December 2000.

184. **Weisser** (Christian R) and **Walker** (Janice R). Electronic Theses and Dissertations: Digitizing Scholarship for Its Own Sake. *The Journal of Electronic Publishing*. 3, 2; December 1997. http://www.press.umich.edu/jep/03-02/etd.html

185. **Wilkin** (A). Some comments on the information broker and the technological gatekeeper. *ASLIB Proceedings*. 26; 1974; 473-482.

186. **Wolf** (Connie) and **Holland** (Douglas). Digitizing and Preserving Plant Images: Linking Plant Images and Databases for Public Access. *First Monday*. 5, 6; June 2000. http://firstmonday.org/issues/issue5_6/wolf/

187. **Yovits** (M C) *et al.* Information Flow and Analysis: Theory, Simulation, and Experiments. 1. Basic Theoretical and Conceptual Development. *Journal of the American Society of Information Science*. May 1981; 187.

188. **Zia** (Lee L). Growing a National Learning Environments and Resources Network for Science, Mathematics, Engineering, and Technology Education: Current Issues and Opportunities for the NSDL Program. *D-Lib Magazine*. 7, 3; March 2001.

189. **Zipf** (H P). Human Behavior and the Principle of Least Effort. Cambridge, Massachussets. Addison-Wesley.

# Index

**Q**



**R**



**S**